WHAT'S THE PLAN?

Your Pain, God's Purpose

B R A D   L E R O Y

WESTBOW
PRESS®
A DIVISION OF THOMAS NELSON
& ZONDERVAN

WestBow Press books may be ordered through booksellers or by contacting:

WestBow Press
A Division of Thomas Nelson & Zondervan
1663 Liberty Drive
Bloomington, IN 47403
www.westbowpress.com
844-714-3454

ISBN: 979-8-3850-2612-8 (sc)
ISBN: 979-8-3850-2613-5 (e)

Library of Congress Control Number: 2024910470

Print information available on the last page.

WestBow Press rev. date: 07/01/2024

To Heidi, Logan and Lexa,
who have travelled this road with me:

I love you and could never have made this journey without you.

CONTENTS

ACKNOWLEDGMENTS

In the pages that follow, I will share some details of my own journey through pain, when I found myself asking, "What's the plan?" One of the things I discovered along the way, is how many people chose to walk this road with me and my family. They didn't have to make this choice, but they did. It would be impossible to adequately express my appreciation without leaving someone out, so I won't try. What I will do is to take this opportunity to share my deepest gratitude to all those over many years who reached out in prayer or with a note, card, email, text, gift, or hospital visit, or who provided needed help at just the right time. I will never forget the sacrifices that so many people have made.

I would also like to thank Larry Moore for reviewing this book before its submission. Larry is a lifelong friend with whom I have had the privilege of sharing many seasons of life and ministry, whose insight, wisdom, encouragement and support have helped guide me along the way.

To Alison Moore, who graciously took time to help put this book together, including helpful content suggestions and editing, I am truly grateful. Alison is a close friend who's very familiar with the details of my story. Her knowledge of my life and the time and personal giftedness that she gave towards this project has allowed this book to be the best possible.

Of my wife, Heidi, and our kids, Logan and Lexa, who have had to endure more than they should have, beyond what seems reasonable or fair, I can only say that their love and faithfulness to God and to me is one of the greatest gifts any person could ever receive. I will never, ever take their love and support for granted. On the many days I did not feel like carrying on, it was their encouragement that often kept me going. I love them for ensuring that I would never have to walk one day of this road alone.

THE LORD'S PRAYER

Our Father in heaven, hallowed be your name,
Your kingdom come, your will be done, on earth as it is in heaven,
Give us today our daily bread.
And forgive us our debts, as we also have forgiven our debtors.
And lead us not into temptation, but deliver us from the evil one.
For thine is the kingdom, and the power, and the glory, for ever.
Amen.

INTRODUCTION

I did not ask to write this book, and to be honest, I'm not confident anyone will read it. Why are you reading this book? I thank you, but I can't tell you that you should. The journey ahead will be far from easy. What follows is not a leisurely morning read with your favorite cup of coffee. It's more of a "roll up your sleeves and let's get to work" kind of book. As the author, I might even tell you to stop reading right now. Why? If you're intrigued by this book, it's probably because things are not going well for you. The problems and challenges in your life seem overwhelming, maybe even insurmountable, and you are desperately looking for answers you cannot find. Every day you're asking the question, "What's the plan?"

If I've just described you, please know how very sorry I am that you are facing all of these challenges. But the truth is that you are the very person I felt compelled to write this book for, with the hope that just maybe, with God's help, you will be able to navigate the challenges in your life at a higher level.

Before we go farther, let me be clear about what we're going to talk about. We're going to talk about pain. There, I said it. Pain. It's one of the realities of life. If you live long enough, some level of pain, in some area of your life, will find you. And when it does, many people are tempted to ask why. "Why am I having to face what I'm experiencing? It's not fair that I have to go through what I am." It's a fair and natural question to ask, I'll give you that, but it's the wrong question. If you ask why for too long, you will just end up in the same place you're already in, with the same problems to solve. What happens if you're never able to answer the question of "Why?" Where does that leave you? It may leave you confused, frustrated, and disillusioned. Those are terrible places to end up, let alone live in. Nothing good ever comes from prolonged seasons in those places.

The much better question to ask is, "What's the plan?" I understand that at first glance it's not really the question you want to ask when you're experiencing the pain of life. It can take some time to move from *why* to *what*. When we ask why, we often receive what we're looking for from ourselves and others. Sympathy. Empathy. Social media allows us to share our pain and receive an immediate shot of support, love, care and concern from others. We have days of not wanting to get out of bed and go on. And for a time, all of this might help take the pain away. But as days, weeks, months, and years go by, you discover that nothing has answered the deepest questions related to the pain you're experiencing. None of your problems were actually solved this way.

It's only when we move from *why* to *what* that we begin to gain traction. It's where we discover that when it comes to pain, we can actually do more with the what than with the why. This is the moment when you give God complete control of everything in your life, when pain is no longer in the driver's seat and forward momentum can begin to happen again. You don't always need to know "Why". God never promises that you will always know "Why" you're facing the specific pain or challenge you're experiencing. What you need to know is, "What's the plan?" How cruel would it be for God not to tell us *what* we need to do, especially when we don't know or can't see the why behind what we're facing?

In the pages that follow, we will explore the question "What's the plan?" when we experience the pain of life. I will share some of my own personal experiences as we discover some answers to this question through the life of Job and the Lord's Prayer. What I won't try to do is explain why pain and suffering exist in the first place.

That's a problem for Genesis, chapter 3, when humankind decided not to listen to God's instructions, and sin, evil, and pain entered into the world. I also won't be talking about the consequences we suffer when we choose to disobey what God told us to do. If you can identify that your suffering is directly caused by a decision you made, that is a much different conversation from the one we will be having. Others have offered explanations on the subject of willful sin and that material is widely available.

Our focus is going to be much narrower. The truth is, sometimes pain happens in life and there is no reasonable explanation for it. The person suffering did nothing to cause the pain they are experiencing. In fact, the opposite argument could be made. There are times when individuals are doing everything they know to be right and still find themselves in a season of suffering. That's the pain I'm talking about.

This pain can come in many forms. Financial. Emotional. Health. When that happens, the question should not be "Why is this happening?" The question should always be "What's the plan?" And honestly, that's what you really need to know and focus on. You don't always have to know why, but what you do need to know is what to do. What do I do with what I'm facing, which I can't make sense of and which I see no purpose or value in? And please hear me on this: God is always faithful to help us know what we need to do when pain affects our lives. When you can't make sense of what you're facing, and you see no value or purpose in it, focus on what God wants you to do.

The warning here is that if you believe you always have to know why things are happening in order for God to be faithful, you will be sadly disappointed. But if you can set aside your compulsive desire to always know why, you can actually discover how to live under the difficulties and pain of life.

CRUCIAL GUIDELINES

Jesus answers the question "What's the plan?" throughout the Lord's Prayer, the prayer He taught His disciples to pray. But centuries before this prayer was ever given, Job lived it. Revisiting Job's life puts flesh on the skeleton of the prayer that Jesus eventually teaches. Job is often known as the "suffering servant" who endured much pain. Years before Jesus taught His disciples how to pray, Job had to figure out the big questions of life. At critical moments, he would ask, "What's the plan?" In my own journey of life and ministry, I too have asked this question. And it wasn't because *I* didn't have a plan—I had a plan, or at least I thought I did. In a position of leadership, we feel immense pressure always to have a plan. In the absence of a plan, we'll make one up, just to say we have a plan. But at crossroads filled with pain, it can quickly become obvious that the leader has no idea what the plan is or should be. These difficult and painful moments are also the ones where God seems to show up and do some of His best work! I don't fully understand why that is, but I've found it to be true. My encouragement to you is to make peace with not always having to know the "why" behind everything that may happen in life. If *why* becomes the focus, pain becomes paralyzing. If *what* becomes the focus, pain can turn into purpose.

Before we go any farther, I need to share two important guidelines.

1. **Pain does not come in a specific order.** As I unpack Job's pain, along with my own, you may notice that I don't follow Job's life in chronological order, because your pain might not arrive in the same order as it did for Job—mine didn't. And you may not experience all the pain in life, or the same kinds of pain, that Job did. I hope you don't! But it's very likely that you will experience at least some of the pain that Job did. When you do, Job's example can serve as a guide through these moments of life.

2. **The Lord's Prayer should be prayed in the order it was given.** At some level, we deal with each of the areas covered in the Lord's Prayer *every day*. Jesus taught His disciples to pray this prayer in a specific order. No matter where you are in life, always pray all the prayer in the order in which it was given. At the same time, you may need to "camp out" in one part of the prayer over others because of what you're facing at any given time. That's OK. For example, if you're worried about making ends meet, you might spend more time praying for God's provision of daily bread. But you should daily pray all of the prayer that Jesus gave.

So if are you still interested in diving into the question "What's the plan?" please understand that while the journey may be challenging, the destination will be worth it.

CHAPTER 1

WHO'S IN CHARGE?

Our Father in heaven, hallowed be your name.

MATTHEW 6:9 NIV[1]

The first thing that needs to be settled in life, especially when we experience the pain of it, is who's in charge. If we're going answer the question "What's the plan?" when it comes to pain, someone ultimately has to be in charge and have the answer. Who's it going to be? If you're like most people, the temptation will be to start with the wrong source. Our natural tendency is to look in all the wrong places, among all the wrong people, in the moment we face the pain of life.

How often have you heard of someone who chose to listen to the wrong person, especially during one of the hardest moments of their life? Those stories are filled with regret and usually even more pain. I've worked with people long enough to have heard this line too many times to count: "If I could only go back and do that over again. I wish I had never listened to that person." Sigh. Inside, I hurt with them and wish the very same thing for them. And truth be told, I could share my own stories of making this exact same mistake.

Out of all the sermons ever preached, Jesus gave the most famous

---

[1] Unless otherwise noted, all quotations from the Bible are from the New International Version (NIV).

one, the Sermon on the Mount (Matthew 5–7). Jesus may have taken several days to teach this message—so give your pastor a break for running a few minutes over now and then!—and tucked away in the middle of it, we find Jesus teaching His disciples to pray. It's as if after teaching about some important areas of life and faith, Jesus had said, "By the way, before I go any farther, none of this is going to be easy. Don't try and do any of this by yourself. You don't have to go it alone. In fact, I'm recommending that you don't!"

Jesus knew exactly what His followers were going to face in life. He knew that at times life would be difficult. Pain would be involved. If you follow the lives of Jesus' disciples through to completion, it's hard to make the argument that their earthly lives improved after choosing to follow Jesus. One might even say that their earthly lives were better before they made that decision—unless you consider ridicule, imprisonment, torture, and death to be an improvement, which Jesus' disciples and many of His followers would live to experience.

In recent years, I have been bothered by the sanitized version of Christianity the church has often offered. The idea that your earthly life improves when you choose to follow Jesus doesn't seem to square with scripture or reality. On the front end, it's definitely much easier to sell—*just don't read the fine print.* And in one sense, it does improve. Jesus is now with you, and His power and strength are available to you.

But have you asked yourself why His power and strength are needed in the first place? It's because you're being invited into a life that won't always be easy! There is a greater mission going on than you can see, taste, touch, or smell, and you are being invited into it. There will be moments when you will be in over your head if left on your own. Life will not always seem fair. Pain will be part of the journey.

What's also interesting is that Jesus says the example of prayer they have seen modeled by others is not the one they should follow. In the verses that lead up to the Lord's Prayer, Jesus says in effect, "Don't pray to be seen by others! Don't babble on like you hear others doing! Yes, you need to pray, but the current examples are not ones you should follow." It's only then that Jesus says, "This, then, is how you should pray" (Matthew 6:9 NIV). In other words, "Now that I've cleared up what *not* to do, here's what you *should* do."

The opening line to the Lord's Prayer is "Our Father in heaven, hallowed be your name" (Matt. 6:9 NIV). When you learn to pray this opening line, you will have answered the all-important question, "Who's in charge?" The answer is our Father in heaven. It's not you. It's not your family. It's not your friends. The person who is in charge is your Heavenly Father. So that's why the first issue that needs to be settled when it comes to pain is, "Who's in charge?"

And be careful with this one, because I'm guessing that much like me, you were led to believe that you are in charge. If you work hard enough, roll up your sleeves, and solve enough problems, then everything will be all right. But what happens when you face problems that are far beyond your capacity to solve, or are experiencing a level of pain you can't explain? I can't state this strongly enough: the time to settle the question of who's in charge is *before* you find yourself in this situation. There is way too much going on to answer this question in the moment pain shows up.

There are two important things you need to know about your Heavenly Father.

1. You have a Heavenly Father.

The first thing to grab hold of is that you have a Heavenly Father! On the surface, this seems simple enough. But when you realize that God, the creator of all things, who rules the world, is also your father, that is a mind-blowing moment! That realization is one that should never grow old.

What makes the opening of this prayer even more incredible is that it was not normal for the Jews of that day to call God "Father"— it would have been considered far too intimate or casual. It would have been more natural for them to conclude, "I know God. I know who He is, but we're not exactly on a first-name basis." But from the outset, Jesus removes this line of thinking by inviting us to call God our Father. As followers of Jesus, we have a father in heaven who is available to us, especially in the desperate and painful times of life. Jesus isn't just saying, "This is how I talk to God, who is my father." He's saying, "This is how you should talk to God too!" Is there ever a time of greater need for your Heavenly Father to be not distant but close, to be a simple word away, than the time of pain?

Jesus is saying something else of great importance when He tells His disciples to pray to "our Father." In using the word "our," Jesus is saying that you can pray to the same Heavenly Father as He does, but He's also saying, "You have brothers and sisters who also have learned to pray this same way and can be of help to you during your moments of pain." You are part of God's family, with all the help, resources, and connections available through that family!

Especially in moments of pain, I have found that God working through the family of God made all the difference. Don't waste time with people who mean well but have not learned to pray this way. You will just add to your pain. Find others who share the same Heavenly Father as you do and pray together the way Jesus taught His disciples to pray.

2. Your Heavenly Father is Holy.

Let me take a moment to underscore what so many others have communicated about our Father in heaven. God is Holy. He's set apart. He's a God of love. He's a good father who loves you. Regardless of whatever picture you may have of a father, God is the best father you will ever have. Not only that, He wants what's best for you. And this is where it gets tricky. Because if it's true that God wants what's best for us—and it is—then what's with all the pain? What's the plan for that? I'm sympathetic to this question, but for now, here's what you have to lock down: you and I have a Heavenly Father who understands what we don't.

Take a moment. Breathe. I know you feel that you have to know, or that you actually do know, everything that is happening.

You don't. You just don't. If those are your toes I just stepped on, I apologize—I'm dancing around some difficult truth, and I was never good at dancing. It's why I keep stepping on toes. If you don't accept this truth, you will struggle, especially during times of pain. Many refuse to accept that God knows what we don't. To some it seems like the coward's way out. "Just believe *because*," and they don't buy it. The life lived by faith is not for the faint of heart. It's difficult. But once we accept that we don't know everything we think we do, we can choose to do the hardest thing we may ever have to do: trust that our Heavenly Father, who is holy, is actually the one in charge.

The temptation in life, especially in moments of pain, is to make everything about us. Not only will that not solve anything, it will actually make things worse. Being obsessed with oneself, even when it seems warranted, is always a dangerous way to behave—unless, of course, you actually *are* able to answer all the questions of life (spoiler alert: you aren't). It makes much more sense for us to focus our attention on our Father in heaven who is holy, who understands what we don't, and who has all the real answers we need.

JOB SETTLES WHO'S IN CHARGE

Long before Jesus offered the Lord's Prayer, Job lived it. Having no idea of what he was about to face, with no storms or pain on the horizon, Job settled who was going to be in charge of his life. The opening verse in the book of Job says:

> In the land of Uz there lived a man whose name was Job. This man was blameless and upright; he feared God and shunned evil. (Job 1:1)

What I want to emphasize is not that Job was blameless and upright or that he feared God and shunned evil. What I want to emphasize is that Job settled the question of who's in charge *before* he experienced all the pain he would face.

Everyone cries out to God in the moment of pain. It's a cry of desperation, a pleading to have an overwhelming and painful circumstance resolved. That inclination is as natural as breathing. The problem is that it's too late to cultivate the kind of relationship you need with your Heavenly Father as you're experiencing the pain of life. It's much better to have a growing relationship with your Heavenly Father in advance of difficult and painful seasons.

Job knew he had a Father in heaven who was holy, and even when life was good, this relationship was Job's number one priority. Job also knew what it meant to be a father. I would imagine that Job's relationship with his Heavenly Father shaped the relationships he had with his own children, seven sons and three daughters (Job 1:2). He owned 7,000 sheep, 3,000 camels, 500 oxen, and 500 donkeys and had a large number of servants (Job 1:3). Life was going well for Job at the time we're introduced to him—the part of faith we all like and want. It's easy to preach and sell to others.

But before we're through the first chapter of Job, we learn that Job's sons would have feasts in their homes and invite their sisters to eat and drink with them. Job tried to do everything he could to follow the example of his Father in heaven, who was holy, so after these feasts, Job would send them all to be purified. He would offer a sacrifice for each of them, saying, " 'Perhaps my children have sinned and cursed God in their hearts.' This was Job's regular custom" (Job 1:5b). If you're a parent, you might be thinking, "That's not a bad idea!"

And why did Job do this? Why did he go to the trouble of ensuring that his kids were purified, paying the cost to offer these sacrifices again and again? Job did this because he knew who was in charge! He knew exactly who he was following, his Father in heaven, who is holy. We're also told that Job "was the greatest man among all the people of the East" (Job 1:3). This statement could be true of Job only if he had first settled who was in charge. It wasn't because

Job was perfect. He wasn't. Job was as human as you and I are. Job was blameless because he had settled the question of who would be in charge and consistently made that his focus. Before this decision would be put to the test, it was settled. Job's Father in heaven would be the one who was in charge, always. End of question.

Later in the story, we're told what Job did with all the blessings he had received from God before he experienced pain. We're told he rescued the poor; took care of those who were sick, disabled, or dying; and was a father to orphans (Job 29:12–17). If that was not enough, Job would use his influence in court against those who took advantage of others, especially those who could not defend themselves (Job 31:16–21). It's not just what you say, it's what you do that shows who's in charge. God blessed Job because He could also fully trust Job with these blessings.

THE DECISION: GOD WILL BE IN CHARGE

As a high school student growing up in Toronto, I truly sold out to Jesus. I knew He was who He said he was. In fact, I believed it so much that at a summer camp meeting I felt called into ministry to give my earthly life in service to God. I was excited about the opportunity to serve. And for the first ten years (1993–2003), things were great. It seemed liked everything was coming together. I met my incredible wife, Heidi. I went to Bible college to be trained for ministry. God opened up many doors during this time, including going on my first mission trip to Peru.

When I graduated, I wasn't sure exactly what God had next for me and was feeling unsettled. Then an opportunity opened up to work with youth and youth leaders across North America. I moved to Indianapolis, where I have lived ever since. This opportunity allowed me a wide variety of experiences, including working with some incredible leaders, youth conventions, leadership training and short-term missions trips. I traveled around the country and around the world. To me, I was living "Our Father in heaven, hallowed be your name." It was going to be smooth sailing from here on out. If this is what life and ministry is, then I'm fully in! Sign me up!

But as life and ministry continued, it would not always be this way. Things were going to get more challenging than I ever could have imagined. When pain began to show up in my life in various ways, the question I was going to have to answer was, "Will God still be my Father in heaven? Will His name still be hallowed or holy to me?" It's easy to pray this when things are going well! It's easy to say, "God, I will claim you as my Heavenly Father who is all powerful and holy, just as long as you bless me and do what I think you should!" But when things get tough, this question gets put to the test. Don't get me wrong. When life and ministry were good, I prayed this prayer and meant it. It just didn't become real to me until this truth was challenged by the pain of life.

So let me ask you, who's in charge of your life? Be honest, who is it? Settle this question first. Stop praying until you do. If you don't, when pain arrives, you will end up praying all the wrong things. "God, get me out of this. God, make it stop. God, why are you allowing these things to happen?" Now, you might be thinking, "But didn't Job pray those very kinds of things?" He absolutely did! He also had to go back to God and apologize for doing so, especially for calling the character of God into question. As understandable as these prayers are, they are not the right ones when pain surfaces. Let me go one step farther and say that if there is any doubt that you have a Father in heaven, who is holy, when pain shows up you will be in trouble. You will conclude He must not really be in charge or you would not be facing all that you're having to go through. And if he's not really "our" Father, then I guess I'm going to just have to go it alone.

The opening line of the Lord's Prayer settles the question, "Who's in charge?" This question has to be answered before pain arrives. There is pre-work to handling pain! You can't do all of this in the moment of pain. When pain shows up, there's way too much going on to answer this question. And if you're unsure about how you would answer, pain will clarify that for you. It's often been said that we show who we really are when we're under pressure. Pressure also answers the question, "Who's in charge?" It did for Job. It did for me. It will for you.

So to answer the question "What's the plan?" start by praying: "Our Father in heaven, hallowed be your name …"

CHAPTER 2

YOUR WAY OR HIS WAY?

Your kingdom come, your will be done,
on earth as it is in heaven.
MATTHEW 6:10 NIV

O ne of the places where pain gets confusing is when we highlight the here and now (on earth) over the then and there (heaven). We are so fixated on all that is happening right now that we start to elevate its importance beyond the larger purpose God is fulfilling. In other words, everything going on in our world is not ultimately what it's all about. There is a spiritual reality to life. It can't just always be about what's in front of us. Intuitively, as believers, we know this to be true. We share this truth with others. But as we live life, problems begin to surface. Pain shows up. And it's in those moments that we forget to pray the next line of the Lord's Prayer, "Your kingdom come, your will be done, on earth as it is in heaven" (Matt. 6:10 NIV). It's one thing to pray, "Our Father in heaven, hallowed be your name." It's a completely different thing to pray, "Your kingdom come, your will be done, on earth as it is in heaven."

Let me take this moment to remind you that the Lord's Prayer must be prayed in the order it was given. Order matters. God must first be our Heavenly Father who is holy, if we have any chance at praying that His will be done on earth as it is in heaven. But if we've answered the first question of who's in charge? correctly, shouldn't the second part of the prayer come naturally?

JOB'S GOOD OLE DAYS

Job had already determined that God would be in charge of his life. Even with the strain and sacrifice of living to follow God's instructions as carefully as he could, there is no question that Job was living a blessed life. He had a family. He had more than he needed. He was respected and admired by everyone. How hard is it to claim God as being the one who is in charge of your life when things are going that well? Of course he followed God! Why wouldn't he? Who wouldn't follow God if life was good times all the time? I can't imagine praying any way other than "Your kingdom come, your will be done, on earth as it is in heaven," if what I'm experiencing means all of that! In fact, I'd like even more of your kingdom to come, and your will to be done, right here, right now! But as they say, be careful what you ask for.

If God is the one in charge, then it always has to be about His kingdom. It has to be about His will. But hold on a second. Are you absolutely sure you know what God's kingdom is all about? Are you confident that you know what His will is? I'm not asking whether you have any ideas about what you think God's will should be for your life. I'm not asking whether you have all the answers you think God should have for whatever you're facing. I'm asking, are you fully submitted to whatever it means for God's kingdom to come and His will to be done on earth as it is in heaven? Are you prepared for what that might mean for you? Does your answer allow for God to use pain to accomplish His purposes here on earth?

GOD'S WILL ON EARTH: NOT A NEW PROBLEM

This is not a new problem for believers. Since the beginning of time, those who claim to believe in God have tried to tell God what they believe His will and purpose should be. It's easy to put God in charge of our life when we're also happy to tell Him what we think His purpose and will ought to be, or when we've concluded that all God's will means is that we will have earthly health, wealth, great relationships and everything this world has to offer. It gets a little more challenging when we find out what it really means.

Adam and Eve struggled with this whole concept. They knew God. They followed God. They were blessed by God. God was their Heavenly Father, and all He asked was that they do not do one thing. How hard could that be? But if it's about God's kingdom coming here on earth as it is in heaven, do you understand what that implies? It implies that there is another kingdom at work that is at odds with God's kingdom. To state it more strongly, it is a kingdom that is at war with God. So, when the serpent comes to Eve in the garden and asks, "Did God really say you must not eat from the tree that is in the middle of the garden?" (Genesis 3:3), what He's saying is, "Are you really all about God's kingdom and will being done here on earth as it is in heaven?"

The Israelites, God's chosen people, continually tripped over defining God's kingdom and will here on earth inaccurately. (And they had a lot of time to wander around and sort it out—forty years to be exact.) By the time Jesus came, genuine followers of God still hadn't figured out how to pray this prayer related to God's kingdom, will, and purpose being done here on earth. Their prayers and desires focused on wanting the nation of Israel to be restored to its rightful place, and it would have also been OK with them if Rome got what was coming to them too.

But Jesus began to talk about a kingdom that was not of this world. About treasure in heaven. He would add to that the whole idea of picking up your cross and following Him. At one point, Jesus instructed His followers to count the cost to follow Him. Count the cost? What in the world is Jesus talking about? I thought it was only "count your blessings," not "count the cost." All these things Jesus said were not what the people wanted to hear. It was not what they were looking for. Eventually, Jesus went to the Cross and gave His life. Jesus's earthly life was one of every imaginable pain possible, including crucifixion, encouraged by the very ones who claimed to follow God in the first place. Nevertheless, God's purpose has always been an invitation to join God in His kingdom forever, where there will be no more pain and suffering. If pain here on earth is involved in order to accomplish this purpose, so be it.

Right before going to the Cross, Jesus prays this prayer: "My Father, if it is possible, may this cup be taken from me. Yet not as I will, but as you will" (Matthew 26:39). The example here is so rich and deep that it's hard to wrap our minds around it. Jesus, who is the Son of God, who *is* God but who is also fully human, is praying to His Father in Heaven that God's will would be done. The divine side of Jesus didn't need to pray this, but the earthly side certainly did.

Jesus being both God and man is an amazing concept to try to understand. Can you picture the inner conflict? Which side, the earthly or the heavenly, was going to win out in this moment? It's the same conflict you experience at a much lower level in your greatest moments of pain. You believe in God, your Heavenly Father, and you want His will to be done, but you're also human, and the pain in front of you is not something you want to face. Now, what was being asked of Jesus was something only He could do—only Jesus could serve as the sinless sacrifice for us. But that doesn't mean that God won't ask *you* to do something that only you can do.

In His deepest moment of earthly pain, Jesus prays to His Heavenly Father, who is holy, that somehow what He was being asked to do might be accomplished some other way. Fair enough. That's the part of the prayer that makes sense to us! But to pray "not my will, but yours be done" is at a level that stretches our hearts and minds to understand. Even when we do settle that Jesus actually did pray this prayer and follow through on what God was asking Him to do, we then conclude that was something only Jesus needed to pray. That was for Him, not for us. Let me ask you, have you ever found yourself in a moment of pain, having to pray the same prayer? Have you ever gone to this deeper place that would submit to God's will, no matter what, regardless of the cost or pain required, knowing that His will is first and foremost, the most important consideration?

HEAVEN AND EARTH COLLIDE

As Job is living out his life, doing the very best he can to follow God, other conversations were beginning to happen—conversations that he was not aware of. The heavenly realm was working overtime, and Job didn't even realize it yet! The same is absolutely true for us. You may not fully be aware of it. You can't physically see or hear these conversations, but they are happening. I know you think it's all about today, this week, this month, or this year. It's not. The biggest thing going on is God's will being done on earth as it is in heaven. It's not your will being done on earth, and who cares about heaven? I know, I know. You're offended. I understand that I might not be telling you everything you want to hear. Having said that, please know my heart is to share what I believe to be true and of help to you!

The question of God's kingdom and will being done on earth, more specifically in the life of Job, is about to get real. In the first chapter of Job, we're not even past verse 6 when we're told of a conversation between God and Satan. The enemy, Satan, has been roaming the earth, going back and forth in it. In this moment, God poses a question to Satan: "Have you considered my servant Job? There is no one on earth like him; he is blameless and upright, a man who fears God and shuns evil" (Job 1:8b). Have you ever read that and thought, "Come on, God! Job is one of the good guys! Why would you bring him up to Satan? Leave him alone! If that's what it means to follow you, then I'm not so sure about all of this."

Have you ever been in a conversation where both sides try to "one-up" each other? "Oh yeah? Well, what about—" So Satan responds exactly the way you think he would. "Give me a break, God! You bless him and protect him. Why would he not serve you? But if you allowed him to suffer, to feel some pain, I bet you it would be a different story!" God plays along and tells Satan that he can do whatever he wants to Job—he just can't touch his life. Considering what's about to happen, we can take this as good news. The reality is that God is always in control, sets all the parameters, and won't allow anything He doesn't want to happen. When you find yourself in the middle of suffering that seems to make no sense, that reality is a place of peace.

And now we get to the part of the story where everything is about to go wrong for Job. In a matter of a few short verses, he loses everything. All of his oxen, donkeys, sheep, and servants—gone. Camels—gone. His sons and daughters were doing what they did, feasting and drinking, when a mighty wind came up. The house collapsed on them, leaving all of them dead. And how did Job respond? He says, "Naked I came from my mother's womb, and naked I will depart. The Lord gave and the Lord has taken away; may the name of the Lord be praised" (Job 1:21b).

Do you know what Job means when he says, "The Lord gave and the Lord has taken away; may the name of the Lord be praised"? He's saying, "Your kingdom come, your will be done, on earth as it is in heaven." How many followers of God start by praying to their Heavenly Father, only to stop short of praying that His will be done when things get hard? This is the difficult reality of faith.

There was nothing easy about any of this for Job. The danger in this story would be concluding that the truth that Job lived and experienced doesn't apply to us. It's just another great Bible story for us to marvel at how a hero of the faith handled pain and suffering. But I promise you, if you live long enough and follow closely enough, pain and suffering will enter into *your* story. The book of Job does not answer the question "Why do good people suffer?" The book of Job answers the question "What do good people do when they suffer?"

As soon as Job thinks his season of pain is over, a second round begins. Chapter 2 of the book of Job starts almost exactly as chapter 1 ends. Reading along, you might think there's some kind of printing error. God poses the same question to Satan: "Have you considered my servant Job? There is no one on earth like him; he is blameless and upright, a man who fears God and shuns evil" (Job 2:3a). You may be thinking, "If the plan is to pray to God for His will to be done, and that's the result, no thanks!" That's a reasonable conclusion to come to, if you think that God's purpose in heaven and on earth is to remove all the pain from your life. How could the plan of a good and loving God include my pain? Makes no sense. But if you've settled that God's plan is to invite everyone into a relationship with Him that will last forever, then you can begin to consider how the pain you're facing might play into that plan. And this second test that Job will face goes to a whole other level.

Satan basically says to God, "Job continues to serve you because you have spared him any physical pain. Yes, you have allowed him to lose everything he has, but if you were to allow physical suffering, Job will curse you to your face." This is the moment when God does the unthinkable and actually agrees to allow Satan to inflict physical suffering on Job. The only condition that God places on Satan is that he must spare Job's life. Within those parameters set by God (again, the great news is that even when you're suffering, God is the one who sets the limits), Satan inflicts suffering from the top of Job's head to the soles of his feet (Job 2:7). It was so bad that Job sat and scraped his sores with a piece of broken pottery.

Isn't enough, enough? All of us can handle a certain amount of suffering. We understand that life sometimes is not easy, but when it rises to a certain level, most people respond with, "Enough! I can't take anymore!" So how do you think Job responded? In an amazing display of consistency, Job responds to both of these tests in exactly the same way. We are told that after the first test, "In all this, Job did not sin by charging God with wrongdoing" (Job 1:22). After the second test, "In all this, Job did not sin in what he said" (Job 2:10b).

It's one thing to accept what we don't want to accept from God, but it's a whole other thing not to blame God for what we're facing. Job does not allow himself to hold God responsible for any of the things he faced. I'll be honest: I have a hard time with this one. How does Job not allow himself to lay all that he has endured at God's feet? I wouldn't have been critical of Job if he had; would you? But he doesn't. Job just doesn't go there. Job had settled that his Father in heaven is holy and that His will was to be done here on earth as in heaven. There is no reasonable explanation beyond that.

If Job had blamed God for his lot in life, then in that moment Job's pain would have been of no use to God's plan and purpose. We would not be talking about him today because his story would not have made it into scripture. How you handle blessings is not what really matters. It's how you handle pain.

In the first chapter of this book, I noted that Job used the blessings God had given him to help others, including not only his family but also orphans and those who were treated unfairly. What a great place to start! But too often we conclude that we'll finish there too, thinking, "I will enjoy the blessings of life and even do some good with it, but let's forget about anything related to pain and suffering." What Job models for us is how to handle both blessing and suffering. Job knew what many people fail to realize: we are in the hands of God, and He can use both blessing and suffering to fulfill His will here on earth. Our responsibility as followers is to pray that His will be done on earth as it is in heaven, regardless of what that might mean for us. The question I ask myself and that I will pose to you right now is, "Could you and I respond in the same way Job did when faced with similar circumstances?"

WHEN THE EARTHLY ROAD GETS ROUGH

In 2006, my wife Heidi and I began to feel God leading us to do something we never thought He would ask of us. After serving in ministry in staff positions for eleven years, within both a ministry organization and then a local church, we felt that God was calling us to start a church. We had lived in Indianapolis most of our married life. Our two children had been born here. We were open to go wherever God might want us to go, but as we began to pray and diligently seek God, we felt called to a growing suburb of Indianapolis that was going to need more churches. The opportunity to get into a newer, growing community and to be part of what God wanted done there was very exciting to us. What could be more in line with God's will being done on earth as in heaven than planting a church? We knew there might be some hard days, but come on—God had to be in this! God's will? New church. New believers. Hand in glove.

In March 2007, we began the journey towards launching Harvest Church with a team of about twenty-five people. We met in our home twice a month for planning, prayer, and relationship building. That summer, we began finding opportunities to serve in the community. In fall 2007, we began holding pre-launch and preview services. Our official launch Sunday was October 14, 2007, at a local elementary school. While there is much that I could share about this time and what it takes to start a church, I'll just provide some context without an exhaustive history.

The first two years of Harvest Church were constant meetings, outreach opportunities, weekly worship, discipleship, and team building. In 2009, after this initial season of starting Harvest, I decided to go back to school to work on my Master of Divinity degree (MDiv) while continuing to pastor Harvest. Our two children, Logan and Lexa, were six and four years old at the time. My wife Heidi also has always worked full-time. Harvest had an ongoing capital campaign to raise funds for our first permanent facility. Needless to say, it was a busy season.

In February 2013, I handed in my last assignment for my MDiv degree, thinking, "Phew! Glad that's over! Now I can focus completely on Harvest and my family." We had worked with an architect to develop plans for the new building, and land had been secured. It was then that problems began to surface. The elementary school we had been meeting in informed us that our annual renewal would not be approved, as they no longer wanted to rent to outside organizations, but we still didn't have the approvals we needed even to break ground for our new home. You may already know this, but you can't just buy land, develop plans, and break ground. Apparently, there are others who have a say in the matter! So we had to confront moving out of our existing home and feeling stonewalled in building our new one—both completely outside our control. For such a new community, there were not many (or any) facilities where we could move the church. When we started Harvest, we knew facilities would be a challenge, which is why we had begun early—we thought—to make plans for a permanent home.

On Sunday, March 17, 2013, I stood up in front of Harvest and shared all this news. We no longer could meet at the school. The building plans we had been working on and raising money towards had stalled out significantly, based on decisions and approvals that were outside our control. I told Harvest that God had not forgotten about us and that He would provide what we need. In my heart I believed what I was saying, but my head was struggling to make sense of it all. Our last Sunday in the school would be on Easter, which was early that year—only two weeks away, on March 31.

That morning was one of the toughest I have ever had, but it wasn't even the worst thing to happen that day. Little did I know, but Sunday, March 17, 2013, would be the last time I would speak at the elementary school, our first church home for Harvest.

After service, we went to lunch with some close friends. While we were eating, I started to feel pain in my right lower abdomen. It kept coming and going, but I finally told Heidi that I thought I needed to go home. We had driven separately to church that day, so she took me to get my car, which was parked behind the school. We live only a couple of miles from the school, but I could hardly make it home. I went upstairs and lay down. Over the next couple of hours, the pain increased to a level I had never experienced before.

My wife called my sister-in-law, who is a nurse. She came over and said, "He's turning gray. We need to get him to the ER right now!"

My ten-year-old son, Logan, stood at the bottom of the stairs as I struggled down. I remember saying to him, "It will be OK, buddy." We dropped off our kids at a friends' house on the way to the ER. I later found out that when they asked Logan if he was doing OK at dinner that night, he turned to them and said, "Could we pray for my dad?"

As we arrived at the ER, I was doubled over. Without asking any questions, they took me straight back and started IV fluids and pain medication. Once I had settled, they began to do some evaluations and tests. It was intestinal. I was transferred to another hospital and started on IV antibiotics. Within two days, my intestine perforated. I was transferred again to another hospital. After two weeks there, I was sent home on a six-week course of IV antibiotics to deal with the infection before my first surgery, which was scheduled for May 2013.

Shortly after I was discharged from the hospital, and before this first surgery, graduation for completing my master's degree took place in April. I remember sitting through the ceremony, walking across the stage, and shaking the hand of the president of the seminary. When it was over, I walked to my car for one of the IV antibiotics that had to be done at certain times of the day. I can only imagine what that looked like! Can you see the headline now? SEMINARIAN SHOOTS UP IN PARKING LOT AFTER GRADUATION.

Over the past ten years, I have had fourteen surgeries, not to mention more hospitalizations, physical therapy, doctor's appointments, and ongoing medical care than I care to go over. Three of the surgeries have taken place at the Cleveland Clinic, the second-best hospital system in the US for gastroenterology. One of the surgeries was the removal of my large intestine. Other issues have since been diagnosed in other areas of my GI tract, including my small intestine and stomach, which now require constant attention. If all of that was not enough, during this same period my gallbladder needed to be removed.

A previous and unrelated injury to my neck also surfaced. The backstory there was that years ago while coaching here in Indiana, I had fallen off the back of a hockey net, suffering contusions on the brain. Per USA Hockey rules, I was not allowed to get up or be helped off the ice and had to wait for paramedics. Apparently, it was quite a scene. Over time, issues in my neck began to develop. So in addition to all the GI problems and surgeries, I ended up having two neck surgeries, including double neck fusion. I still find it humorous that my biggest injury from hockey came not from playing in Canada but from coaching in Indiana!

As I am writing this book, I just had my most recent surgery to have a pain pump implanted. At the end of 2022, I lost 35 to 40 pounds unexpectedly and without trying. Pain and other issues related to eating had started to become a problem. It was determined that the use of a pain pump was my best option to stop losing weight and to try to regain a regular level of diet. I have a home care nurse who comes in on Tuesdays, do a daily IV that takes 3 hours as well as a regular set of doctors' appointments.

Along this road, I have continually found myself asking the question, "What's the plan?" Everything I have mentioned so far on this topic, through the Lord's Prayer and the life of Job, became real to me. It was no longer truth found in the pages of scripture or in the abstract. Pain was front and center and impossible to ignore. Was I going to be able to pray "Your kingdom come, your will be done" if praying that prayer included all of this? Are you able to pray this with all that you're facing in your life? I'll be honest: there have been many days when it was tough to pray this prayer, or I simply refused to pray it altogether, especially when pain began to affect other people in my life. My wife, Heidi. My kids, Logan and Lexa. Friends. Harvest. It's hard to pray for God's will to be done on earth as it is in heaven, while you're looking at how the will of God affects the people you care about the most.

In the middle of Job's pain, Job believes and prays for God's will to be done. That's what he meant when he said, "Naked I came and naked I will depart. The Lord gave and the Lord has taken away.

May the name of the Lord be praised." Now, we know the end of Job's story, but in this moment, he doesn't! And that's the entire point: Job prays this not knowing how it will all work out. All he knows is that he can trust his Heavenly Father who is holy and that he should pray that His will be done on earth as it is in heaven.

Along my own journey, things have not gone the way I thought they would. In fact, things still aren't going exactly how I thought they would go. But I want to tell you something important: I didn't learn to pray and trust God just by growing up in the church. It wasn't enough to study at Bible college. It wasn't even enough to go out and serve in the church. God allowed me to go to a deeper place of trust in Him only when pain showed up that didn't make sense, pain I still don't completely understand. I am not blameless, and I am not comparing myself at all to Job. All I am saying is that when you learn to pray the way Jesus taught us to pray, as lived out in the life of Job, trusting in God's will in heaven to be done on earth however He wants to do it, life does not get easier—but it does get simpler. As the complexity grows, so too does the trust that God is who He says He is and is doing all He said He would. We don't have to know everything that is and is not going on. We don't have to be read into all the details to trust that He's working it all out. This is not simply blind faith. It's a complete trust and reliance that in the end, God's figured out what I will never understand completely this side of eternity.

We've often expressed this idea of God's kingdom being done here on earth to mean that God will only bless and provide. After all, He is a good Father who wants good things for His children, right? God doesn't want us to suffer or experience pain, right? The problem is, God's will is first and foremost that people will come to Him. And that purpose overshadows anything else, including our pain. It did for Job. It did for Jesus. It will for you. To put a finer point on it: your pain just may be part of the plan to accomplish God's purpose.

To answer the question "What's the plan?" you must also pray "Your kingdom come, your will be done, on earth as it is in heaven."

CHAPTER 3

IT'S UP TO ME, RIGHT?

Give us today our daily bread.

Matthew 6:11 NIV

We've spent considerable time talking about God, our Holy Heavenly Father, and His will being done on earth as it is in heaven. And all of this talk can be quite heavy, especially when tied to the pain of life that we may be experiencing. But these realities should be given more time and attention than most people give them. Truthfully, most of us would rather skip over everything we've just talked about and get to the things we're going to talk about next. If you were recommending this book to someone else, you might be tempted to say, "Skip chapters 1 and 2, and just start with chapter 3! It gets much more practical in chapter 3." But if you were to do that, you would be heading into the practical areas of life without understanding the power of God needed to handle those areas. The order in which the Lord's Prayer should be prayed matters, even if the pain of life arrives differently for each of us.

Remember these two things:

1. We have a Holy Heavenly Father who loves us.
2. The most important thing is for God's kingdom and will to be done on earth as it is in heaven.

Everything else that Jesus teaches His disciples related to prayer and life falls under these two critical understandings. Job had settled these two areas *before* the practical areas and pain of life showed up in his life. I discovered this to be true in my own life, and I promise it will work the same for you.

Halfway through the Lord's Prayer, Jesus finally begins to talk about the things we face every day. Not the big picture, deep end of the pool concepts, but the realities of life, where the rubber meets the road for all of us. It's here that Jesus invites His followers to pray for the areas of life where we often feel the greatest need. For some, it might relate to daily needs and provision—we honestly don't have what we need, and it's causing great pain in life. Maybe the pain we're facing has to do with an important relationship that is not going well. We lie awake at night praying that God will do something about this broken relationship and take that pain away. Or our pain might be coming from a place of personal struggle or sin that nobody else knows about, but battles are being lost as you sink deeper into a dark place.

Here is a word of caution. The temptation is to start prayer with the practical. Let that sink in for just a moment. We don't always start praying in the place that Jesus taught His disciples to pray in. Our needs and wants often first fuel our prayers. When we focus more on ourselves than on our Holy Heavenly Father and His will, we then tend to pray more about our will than His. When that happens, we end up heading into the practical areas of life with a limited understanding of how things work and what's really going on. If we're not careful and don't pray things in the right order, we can actually make things worse.

What I'm saying is that our constant obsession with the here and now causes us to pray for our earthly needs or relationships or for how to navigate this life before we even acknowledge the one we're actually praying to, let alone ask that His will be done. Jesus wanted to ensure that His disciples kept first things first. He could have taught them to pray first about the things that may have been more on their mind, but He didn't. When we pray first to our Father in heaven that His will be done on earth as it is in heaven, when we get to the practical areas of life, our prayers will already be more in line with His will. Does that make sense? If I first pray about my needs, then my prayers will be shaped by my will and what I think should happen. If I pray in the order Jesus taught, I'm already on my way to being in line with His will.

That's why Jesus teaches His disciples to pray first to their Holy Father in heaven that His will be done and then finally to pray, "Give us today our daily bread." A modern version of this prayer might be something like, "Jesus, don't you know I need more money, a better job, food for my family and the basic needs of life? Heavenly Father, I need more!" Some of you just woke up and are thinking, "Now we're talking! Give us today what we need!" What Jesus is talking about here is our need for daily provision, not some kind of super spiritual lofty idea that we struggle to wrap our minds around. It's practical and on the ground level! Today I need bread, and Jesus says that I should pray to Him to receive it.

The pain you're experiencing in life might not be physical. It might be financial or material, including the basic needs of life. This reality only heightens when it also affects others in your life that you care about. If others rely upon you and something unexpected happens, you might be able to handle it affecting you, but the impact on others may be too much.

DAILY BREAD AT THE VERY BEGINNING

During biblical times, the need for daily bread was extreme and real. There was no modern technology available to save and preserve food. Daily bread was just that—a daily reality to obtain! So on this practical level, let's understand two things.

1. **God has what you need.** If the pain in your life is based upon what you need, go to the one who can provide and ask! Jesus tells us that's exactly what we should do!

2. **God will give you what you need for today.** Sometimes (not always), God will give you more than you need for the day! Regardless, Jesus taught His disciples to pray each day for their daily bread. If God always gave you more than what you needed, you might stop relying on Him. Praying to God to provide daily bread also means that I am completely dependent on God today. And if I pray that same way tomorrow, based on that very real need, I will be dependent on Him tomorrow, and the day after, and the day after that.

In other words, "It's not up to you!" You are not the source of your own provision, and you should find that reality extremely freeing. The problem is that our culture struggles with relying on anyone else, including God. But when we choose to rely on ourselves first, can we really say that we're about the will of our Holy Heavenly Father being done on earth as it is in heaven?

This concept of daily bread is found all the way back at the beginning of scripture. When God set His people free from slavery in Egypt, they found themselves wandering in the desert, a barren land with very little to offer. They were headed somewhere great, but they weren't there yet and wouldn't be for some time. And do you know how the people felt about this?

> In the desert the whole community grumbled against Moses and Aaron. The Israelites said to them, "If only we had died by the Lord's hand in Egypt! There we sat around pots of meat and ate all the food we wanted, but you have brought us out into this desert to starve this entire assembly to death." (Exodus 16:2–3)

Not only were the people not happy, but they even longed to be back in slavery in Egypt, where at least they ate well and were provided for. That's saying something! When given a choice between freedom or slavery, you're saying you would choose slavery?

The question for the Israelites in the desert was whether they would rely on God for their daily provision or take matters back into their own hands. Their immediate pain was directly related to their need for daily bread. So what does God do?

> Then the Lord said to Moses, "I will rain down bread from heaven for you. The people are to go out each day and gather enough for that day." (Exodus 16:4a)

God has enough of what you need that He can actually rain it down from heaven for you. So do you see why it's important to pray in the order Jesus taught? If you want God's bread from heaven, you first have to acknowledge that He is who He says He is and can do what He says He will do.

This bread from heaven was called manna. One explanation of the word *manna* is that it originated in a question, *man hu*, "What is it?" Have you ever set food down in front of your kids only to be asked, "What is it?" Next time, just tell them, "It's manna! Eat your dinner!"

This provision from God was not like anything the Israelites had seen before.

> When the Israelites saw it, they said to each other, "What is it?" for they did not know what it was. Moses said to them, "It is the bread the Lord has given you to eat." (Exodus 16:15)

Manna was like a fine, flaky frost they found on the ground. The Bible describes it as looking like white coriander seed and tasting like wafers made with honey (Exodus 16:31).

When you receive the bread God wants you to have, it may not be like anything you've ever seen before. It also may not be what you want. Have you ever thought about that? God will give you what you need, but it may not be what you want. Will you be OK with whatever daily bread God happens to provide for you at any given time in your life?

While manna provided for their daily needs, it wasn't exactly what the Israelites wanted. In Numbers 11, we're told that they began to complain and crave other food. Manna wasn't very exciting even though it provided for their daily nutritional needs. Do you see the problem here? A land flowing with milk and honey awaited God's people, but all they could see was the manna right in front of them. As a consequence, this current generation of Israelites who were now living on manna, would never see the promised land or enjoy the fruit of it. They had sinned by not having the faith to believe and take the land as God had instructed them to do. However, if they wanted their children and grandchildren to enter into the promised land, they had to keep going, and that meant more manna today.

Another way to look at this would be to say that milk and honey were on the menu, but they chose manna. Manna was God's faithfulness to His people to provide daily bread despite their disobedience. They could have had nothing based on the choices they had made. The people had disobeyed and been unfaithful. In this moment, why should God have done anything for them? But even as they grumbled and complained, God provided the manna they needed. And manna is always better than nothing.

In the New Testament, Jesus refers to this moment in their history and says something remarkable:

> "I am the bread of life. Your ancestors ate the manna
> in the wilderness, yet they died. But here is the
> bread that comes down from heaven, which anyone
> may eat and not die. I am the living bread that came

down from heaven. Whoever eats this bread will live forever. This bread is my flesh, which I will give for the life of the world." (John 6:48–51)

In the same way that the Israelites were not always happy about the manna God provided, when the Bread of Life came, He wasn't exactly what all the people of His time wanted either. To me it's unbelievable, but some of the people who saw, heard, and experienced Jesus firsthand rejected Him. They wanted more than what they believed Jesus was offering to them. I find that hard to understand, but I also recognize that it's the same reality we experience today. When we pray, "Give us today our daily bread," will we be satisfied with what He provides? What God didn't provide was the pots of meat and all the food they enjoyed in Egypt. He gave them what they needed for that day.

This moment in the wilderness was not the only time we find people in scripture in desperate need of daily bread. In the Gospels, Jesus famously multiplies bread on two different occasions. While that solution defies our sense of what we think is possible, that's what He did! But I want you to catch something important in all of this conversation on daily bread. Jesus always invited people into their own provision. Yes, they had to ask Jesus to provide, but that did not mean they could just sit on the sidelines and do nothing. When Jesus multiplied the bread and the fish, the disciples had to distribute it to the 5,000 gathered and to 4,000 on another occasion. Jesus's first miracle was turning water into wine, but He had others get involved by filling the jars with water. When God provided the manna, He told the people that they were to gather it each day (with the one exception when they were to gather two days' worth on the sixth day so they didn't have to work on the Sabbath). God provided the manna, but the Israelites had to go gather it.

When you pray for God to provide your daily bread, be prepared for Him to ask you to do your part. If you only pray and don't obey, you will still be hungry, which will lead to frustration. But as you do your part to help with your own provision, doing exactly what Jesus tells you to do, what is Jesus doing? Jesus has gone back to heaven to prepare a feast—a land of milk and honey for all eternity. This feast is called the wedding supper of the lamb and is for all those who believe in Him. The only table you should ever want to be at is this one! You may pass by other "tables" with what looks like good food here on earth. But only you can decide whether you will be at God's table for all eternity. While you may have to endure manna on earth, there is a feast waiting for you in heaven. Jesus's plan and purpose on earth will ultimately be fulfilled in heaven, and I promise you, you want to be part of it.

But if you need some hope while living here on earth, let me offer you a second helping of hope in this chapter on daily bread. In the same sermon in which Jesus teaches the Lord's Prayer, Jesus goes on to say:

> "Therefore I tell you, do not worry about your life, what you will eat or drink; or about your body, what you will wear. Is not life more than food, and the body more than clothes? ... So do not worry, saying, 'What shall we eat?' Or 'What shall we drink?' Or 'What shall we wear?' For the pagans run after all these things, and your heavenly Father knows that you need them. But seek first his kingdom and his righteousness, and all these things will be given to you as well." (Matthew 6:25, 31–33)

God knows what you need. Your daily bread is already available for you. But did you catch what Jesus said is our part? We are to seek first His kingdom and His righteousness. Do you see now why Jesus taught His followers to pray in the order He gave? Before you get to your need for daily bread, seek first His kingdom. You may not want to do this first. It will go against your natural tendencies and inclinations. However, if we pray and do things the way Jesus says to, then His provision becomes available, even in the moments of our greatest pain and despair.

JOB'S DAILY BREAD EXPERIENCE

So how does praying "Give us today our daily bread" apply to Job? We've already established that Job was a very prosperous business leader, who was considered the "greatest man among all the people of the East" (Job 1:3). Job's wealth of livestock and servants was measured in the many thousands, but what I want to emphasize is that his seven sons and three daughters were not just a blessing he enjoyed personally but were also a source of his wealth. Job's world depended heavily on agriculture, and children were needed to help with the work of the family business. Job and his entire family modeled what it meant both to be blessed by God for their daily bread and to do their part by working hard. One reason Job offered sacrifices for his kids is that he did not want to live without God's blessing, including the blessings he received through his children. But would this principle still apply now that the pain of life had caught up with Job? Would Job still seek God for his daily bread and provision?

When we fast-forward to the end of Job's story as it relates to God's provision for him, we're told that "after Job had prayed for his friends, the Lord made him prosperous again and gave him twice as much as he had before" (Job 42:10). We'll get back to Job praying for his friends in the next chapter, but for now, I want you to see that God's daily bread provision for Job eventually results in abundance. God doesn't just replace what Job had lost, He doubles it! Now, this is not a promise that God will do for you exactly what He did for Job. All through the story, Job had no idea of how things would work out. This verse at the end of the book of Job simply describes what happened.

And here's the amazing thing: Job would have been faithful *regardless of the outcome.* He knew that God would provide for his daily bread. This principle held true even when Job was suffering. God provided for Job's daily needs somehow, in some way, from the least likely of places. While we don't have all the details of God's daily bread provision for Job during his time of suffering, what we do know is that God provided. Job makes it through this time of pain and into a time of great prosperity.

One of the hardest things in life can be going from having a lot to having a little. Talk to anyone who has experienced that reality, and they will tell you the same thing. Job had suffered unimaginable loss and pain, including the loss of all the wealth that God had blessed him with during the first part of his life. But Job also discovered what the apostle Paul came to learn centuries later:

> I know what it is to be in need, and I know what it is to have plenty. I have learned the secret of being content in any and every situation, whether well fed or hungry, whether living in plenty or in want. I can do all this through him who gives me strength. (Philippians 4:12–13)

We like to quote verse 13. You hear that verse a lot. But you first have to learn verse 12 and what it means to be content in every situation in order to claim verse 13. You can only do all things through God who gives you strength if you have also first learned to depend on Him entirely for your daily bread, regardless of what it may be, at any given time.

THE DAILY BREAD LESSON I HAD TO LEARN

Before I planted Harvest Church, I had been in ministry for eleven years. There was a lesson I had to learn early on related to God's provision of daily bread, if I was ever going to make it through what was coming down the road. My first position of ministry came to a close in the spring of 2004. I was working in a denominational structure whose general conference meets every four years. With changes being proposed at the next general conference in summer 2004, which included a restructuring of departments and my current position no longer being available, I found myself in a season of transition and unsure about what I was to do next.

At the time, my wife Heidi and I had a one-year-old son at home and found out that we were expecting our second child, a daughter. While anticipating a new member of the family is normally an exciting time, I was stressed—excited, but stressed. Facing a change in ministry and employment, I went down the hall to my friend's office to unload my stress. He already knew about the ministry transition, but when I told him that Heidi and I were expecting our second child, it caused an emotional response that I remember to this day. He began to laugh! I mean, laugh out of his mind, uncontrollably. "You're out of a job and you guys are having a baby!" Just when I thought he was done, he would burst out laughing again. And here's the thing: he wasn't wrong. Everything he said I was already thinking. I found myself laughing alongside him. Looking back, I know this laughter was a needed moment of lightness in a difficult season.

Not knowing what else to do, I went to work construction with my brothers-in-law, prepping the foundations of homes on a concrete crew during the summer of 2004. This is funnier than it sounds, as I am not handy in any way, shape, or form! (If you happen to live in one of those homes I worked on that summer, I apologize for any little problems you've experienced due to my handiwork.)

What made my season of transition even more interesting was the contrast that had just taken place for me. Six weeks before starting to work construction, I was in Washington, DC, serving on the National Council for Faith-Based Youth as part of my denominational responsibilities. I sat in a room filled with leaders from across the country, in a building directly across from the Capitol. We were given a private tour of the Capitol, which was an incredible experience. Six weeks later, I was wearing a hard hat, raking sand, and digging dirt in the summer heat. I worked alongside some great people that summer, including the son of the legendary Stanley Cup–winning head coach of the Montréal Canadiens, Jacques Demers. After visiting his dad that summer, he brought me back a signed picture! But while this experience had its own value and it was honest work, it was the wrong work for me. I was no good at it and not called to it.

But then something incredible happened. At the church we were attending at the time, I was asked to serve as executive pastor. The only problem was, they couldn't pay me anything, and it was going to be too difficult to establish any kind of rhythm in the role to continue with the hours of construction work. I didn't go into ministry to make money, but just like anyone else, I have daily bread realities and responsibilities to take care of. So to start this new volunteer role at the church, I switched from construction worker to barista at Starbucks. My hope with Starbucks was to work my way into a higher position quickly. Even with tips and the free pound of coffee they give you as a barista each week, it was going to be hard to make the numbers work.

But then God did something that forever changed the course of my life. God's provision of daily bread was about to show up in a way that I never could have imagined. During a Sunday service in September 2004, it was announced that I would be serving as executive pastor as a part-time volunteer. For a few minutes, I shared my personal story and my excitement about being on the team. At the end of the service, someone who was at church from out of town went up to the lead pastor and said that they felt God was asking them to provide one year's salary so I could start back into ministry full-time. This is the moment in my life when "Give us today our daily bread" took on a whole new meaning. I will never forget that Sunday or the moment the lead pastor came and gave me this news!

And yet to this day, I have never met the person who provided this life-changing, miracle gift.

Before noon on that Sunday in September, God provided a year's worth of daily bread! I could work a whole year on my own and not accomplish what God did in one hour. What I didn't realize at the time was how this lesson was not just for that moment. This lesson that I needed to learn would be vitally important down the road.

As I write this book, I am on a six-month blessing from Harvest. When I had to resign in February 2023 due to my ongoing health challenges, Harvest graciously and unexpectedly gave my family and me a generous gift to provide for us during this time—an extremely generous gift for which I will always be truly grateful and humbled to have received! When this time ends, I'm not sure yet what the next turn in the road will be. I continue to manage many medical issues and appointments. To say I never expected to be in this situation would be an understatement. You don't work to earn two degrees and plant a church only to end up here. But here's the thing: the prayer is "Give us today our daily bread." Not tomorrow. Not next week. *Today.* And I can tell you this: in all the trials and struggles, God has never missed one day of daily bread provision. Not one.

Heidi and I always strive to be obedient to God in all things, to do whatever He asks us to do, whenever he asks us to do it. During the seasons of working construction and at Starbucks, we were faithful to tithe on all income and gave wherever God led us to give. There were many times we felt that we couldn't afford to tithe but then quickly concluded we couldn't afford not to, either. We needed God's daily bread provision. We had seen Him work miraculously before, and we were completely reliant on Him once again. How could we do otherwise? God showed up not only on that miracle Sunday in September, but on many other occasions as well!

Now, I'm not saying you should "give to get from God." That's not how daily bread provision works. I'm saying that if you expect God to provide daily bread, you also have to be obedient to what He asks of you. In the area of finances, the first 10 percent belongs to God. We've never questioned that and have always been faithful to it. I'm not saying that to pat ourselves on the back. I just know that if the pain you're experiencing in life is related to your daily bread needs, you need God's provision, and that happens as you rely completely on Him, including doing all He asks you to do. It's hard to expect God to provide daily bread if you are not first obedient to His instructions. But once you've done all He's asked you to do, then you should absolutely pray to your Heavenly Father for your daily bread.

Answering the question "What's the plan?" must also include praying, "Give us today our daily bread."

CHAPTER 4

I'LL JUST ASK MY FRIENDS

And forgive us our debts, as we also
have forgiven our debtors.

Matthew 6:12 NIV

OK, this is about to get even tougher. (Still reading? I've tried to warn you!) So, I have another question for you: "What's your problem?" Are you offended by me asking you that question? It seems kind of rude of me to be so bold. So if you are offended, good! That's perfect preparation for what Jesus is going to instruct His followers to pray next. Jesus was no stranger to the difficulty of relationships, especially during times of pain. It's why He next teaches His disciples to pray, "And forgive us our debts, as we also have forgiven our debtors."

In life, pain does not just come to us through physical or financial challenges. Sometimes, pain shows up in our lives through relationships. This pain can often blindside us, especially during moments where we are already experiencing some other pain in life. When you're already experiencing physical or financial pain, or both, you might expect that relationships would be vitally important in helping you get through these times. But what happens when relationships go sideways, especially when you're already suffering? What happens when relationships hurt more than they help?

Two Realities of Relationships: Debt and Forgiveness

There are different versions or translations of the Lord's Prayer. I'm sure you're familiar with the version that says, "And forgive us our trespasses as we forgive those who trespass against us." That's the version many of us learned as children growing up. The weight of the translation that uses "debt" rather than "trespass" is a bit heavier but also more accurate. Jesus was speaking with a Jewish mindset that equates sin with debt. When we sin, there is a debt owed. It's not just a trivial "trespass" as if you walked across someone's lawn without asking. You can't just say, "My bad," and move on. When sin enters the picture, the debt is significant and requires forgiveness.

Before Jesus arrived on earth, followers of God sought forgiveness of sin by offering sacrifices of animals. That is how seriously God took the sin debt that was owed! When Jesus came, He became the sacrifice for sin. Jesus's shed blood now took the place of the shed blood of sacrificial animals. Hebrews 9:22 tells us that "without the shedding of blood there is no forgiveness." Much more could be said on this subject, but what we need to understand is the seriousness with which Jews understood sin. If the cost for the debt of sin is shed blood, there is no question of how deep this debt goes.

The Greek word "forgive" here literally means "let go" or "release". If we sin, now forgiveness is available through Jesus's shed blood, through which we are forgiven a debt we could never pay on our own. As followers of Jesus, we should never forget this truth. We sinned. Jesus died. His shed blood is what makes forgiveness possible. And when we ask Jesus to forgive us, He literally lets go and releases this debt.

Here's what we're told in Psalm 103:12–13:

> As far as the east is from the west, so far has he removed our transgressions from us. As a father has compassion on his children, so the Lord has compassion on those who fear him.

Do you see why we must first pray, "Our Father in heaven, hallowed be your name"? In that moment when we realize we've sinned and have to ask for forgiveness, it's incredibly important that we have an accurate picture of the one we're asking forgiveness from. You have a Heavenly Father who loves you and wants to forgive you even more than you want to be forgiven. Your Father in heaven loves you and has compassion for you as His child. If the pain you're experiencing in life is due to sin, He is ready and willing to offer His forgiveness. All you have to do is ask.

Now, why is this important when it comes to relationships and any pain you may be experiencing in those relationships? When we forget how much Jesus forgave us, we will be unwilling to forgive others. And if we are unwilling to forgive someone else, we forfeit God's forgiveness for us. It's as simple as that. Just a few verses later in Matthew 6, Jesus adds to His teaching on the Lord's Prayer:

"For if you forgive other people when they sin against you, your heavenly Father will also forgive you. But if you do not forgive others their sins, your Father will not forgive your sins." (Matthew 6:14–15)

Always start by asking God to forgive your sin debt first. When dealing with others and any relational pain you may be experiencing, never forget how much you were forgiven. You will never be able to forgive someone else if you forget how much you've been forgiven. When dealing with relational issues, always start with yourself. And let me remind you that this is the opposite of how the world operates. The world focuses on self and how we have been wronged, without realizing that we may have also wronged others. Forgiveness is the solution to relational pain; it heals our relationship with God when we're forgiven. When we forgive others as we've been forgiven, it heals our relationships with others.

Let's return to the story of Job. If you thought that his pain could not possibly get any worse, you would be wrong. The reality of Job's pain is about to go much deeper. Job has lost everything. His business. His servants. His children. And now some of the people closest to Job are about to show up and chime in. That makes sense. When people are hurting, other people feel compelled to do something to help. But what we're about to find out is that relationships can hurt as much as they help during times of pain. And the closer the relationships, the truer this can be. While the motivation of well-meaning people may be pure, their objectivity may be skewed, resulting in additional pain. This reality is one that people in pain often are not prepared for, and it catches them completely by surprise.

Jesus understood this truth of relationships better than anyone else. He was no stranger to the disappointment of others. It's why He taught His disciples to pray next, "And forgive us our debts, as we also have forgiven our debtors" (Matthew 6:12).

SHE JUST GETS ME!

The first relationship we need to talk about is Job's relationship with his wife. Is there a closer relationship in life than that of husband and wife? When your spouse hurts, do you not grieve and hurt with them? Do you not want to do all you can to help alleviate their pain and suffering? When Job's wife enters the story, what words of encouragement, love, and support do you think she offers to Job in his greatest moment of pain? Here's what we're told:

> His wife said to him, "Are you still maintaining
> your integrity? Curse God and die!" (Job 2:9)

Doesn't that just warm your heart? Have you ever heard such inspirational words of encouragement, comfort, and love? At first glance, these words seem rather harsh, don't they?

But keep in mind all the loss and sorrow Job's wife has suffered too. It wasn't just Job who lost everything—she did too! Those children who died were hers too. The income they lost was her livelihood as well. And now she had to watch her husband suffer physical pain at a level she could never have imagined.

In this chapter on relationships, we should always keep in mind what others have gone through or are going through. Sometimes the pain we're suffering is harder on others than it is on us. It's quite possible that Job's wife couldn't bear to see her husband continue to suffer. She might have said the things she does out of a heart of incredible love. After losing everything, she finds Job sitting on an ash heap, scraping his sores with broken pottery (Job 2:8). Can you picture that? How would you feel if you were in her shoes? I'm guessing you would feel the same way.

But her question of "Are you still maintaining your integrity?" is eye-opening. Does that imply that she no longer is holding on to her integrity? Has she concluded, "What's the point in maintaining faithfulness to God if that's what's going to happen?" Have you ever found yourself asking the same question in a moment of your greatest pain? Have you ever asked this question of someone going through a season of pain?

How Job replies to his wife's extremely emotional response is truly amazing—a master class in dealing with interpersonal conflict, especially when you're experiencing tremendous pain.

> "You are talking like a foolish woman. Shall we
> accept good from God, and not trouble?" (Job 2:10)

When Job says, "You are talking like a foolish woman," he's not calling her a fool; he's saying that her comments are out of character for her. What Job's saying is, "This is not like you! Why are you saying these things?" Job's response stops short of going after her personally while, at the same time, not ignoring the pain her words are causing him.

When dealing with pain in relationships, always focus on the problem, not the person. This was most likely the hardest moment Job ever had in his relationship with his wife. When he needed her the most, because of her own pain and being so close to the situation, she offered the exact opposite of what he needed. I'm also sure that Job grieved for the pain his suffering was causing his wife. After all, Job loved his wife! Although he was hurt, Job's response to his wife is wrapped in love. "I love you, but I don't understand how you can say the things you are saying. Do we not accept both good and bad from God, as He sees fit?"

Job knew his Heavenly Father and was prepared to accept His will being done on earth as it is in heaven, no matter what. And that's the kind of life the follower of Jesus is called to. That's why it's important always to pray the Lord's Prayer in the order it was given. When you're in pain, other well-meaning people start showing up to help, but sometimes instead of helping, all they do is contribute further to your suffering. Their words and advice, while spoken with good intentions, may run contrary to what you actually need to hear and do. And it's too late in the moment of pain to sort all this out. There's just too much going on in the moment when pain has arrived. Job understood all of this and passes this test with flying colors. Right after the interaction with his wife is one of the times we're told, "In all this, Job did not sin in what he said" (Job 2:10b).

The last chapter of Job tells us that God blessed the latter part of his life more than the first, including having more kids: "And he also had seven sons and three daughters" (Job 42:13). This is the same number of kids that Job had lost during his season of pain. But let me ask you this: who was the mother of these children that God blesses Job with after his season of suffering? Could it have been the same person who told Job to curse God and die in chapter 2? Is it possible that Job and his wife reconciled this pain in their relationship? Truthfully, we don't have a definitive answer, but nowhere does it say that Job's first wife died during this time.

It's quite possible that Job's response to his wife allowed for her own healing in this moment of shared pain.

FOR RICHER, FOR POORER, IN SICKNESS AND IN HEALTH

On August 5, 1995, I stood before family and friends as I was married to my incredible wife, Heidi. Wedding ceremonies often times include the phrase, "For richer or poorer, in sickness and in health." I think when you're younger and have the rest of your life in front of you, you can't fully appreciate what all this might mean. Yes, if you're feeling under the weather, I'll bring you some soup or tea. Yes, if we hit a hard time financially, we'll work together to figure it out. But what happens when it gets really rough?

What if on my wedding day, I'd had the foresight to say to Heidi, "What I mean by 'for richer or poorer' is that there will be a time I'm out of ministry and you're pregnant with one child already. Will that still be cool? Oh, and by sickness, I mean chronically ill with more surgeries and hospitalizations than you could ever think possible. We still good?" When I rewind the tape of our life, I've often wondered what she would have said if she knew what was coming. But here's the amazing thing about Heidi. She has always stood by me through everything! I'm quite certain others would have packed it in by now.

But none of this has been easy for her! As days turned into weeks, weeks into months, months into years, it has been incredibly difficult to see those you care about the most suffer due to the challenges you're facing. Heidi has been the personal help and support I've needed and leaned on; she has had to do much more than was ever reasonable. She works full-time to provide for our family, including our health insurance. As a husband and father, I've been humbled by having to sit on the sidelines when I want to be doing more not just for the kingdom of God but for my family.

In one of our honest moments and conversations, she did say to me, "Why is God allowing this to happen? I don't understand. If this is the way it's going to be, why does He not just take you to be with him?" Now, please understand that she was saying this out of love. She simply did not want to see me suffer anymore. Honestly, it's a fair question when you stop and think about it. It's a question that's also crossed my mind on occasion. And in response, I thought, "What did Job say to his wife again? Is this the moment I should call her a fool? If I remember correctly, this seems like the time I'm supposed to do that!" Upon reflection, that didn't seem like the right thing to say! Maybe I should go with something like, "You're talking like a person who has lost their mind?" That also seemed a little harsh.

You'll be glad to know that I went with, "I hear you. I understand all that you're saying. I hate all of this as much as you do. I love you for standing by me through all of these challenges. I'm trusting that somehow, in some way, God is working His plan and purpose out through all of this, even though we can't see it."

WITH FRIENDS LIKE THAT

And just when you think that Job's suffering, specifically related to relational pain, can't get any worse, three of his friends show up. Their names are Eliphaz, Bildad, and Zophar. Before we get to what these friends do wrong, let's first give them some credit for what they do right.

> When Job's three friends, Eliphaz the Temanite, Bildad the Shuhite and Zophar the Naamathite, heard about all the troubles that had come upon him, they set out from their homes and met together by agreement to go and sympathize with him and comfort him. When they saw him from a distance,

they could hardly recognize him; they began to weep aloud, and they tore their robes and sprinkled dust on their heads. Then they sat on the ground with him for seven days and seven nights. No one said a word to him, because they saw how great his suffering was. (Job 2:11–13)

So, what do these three friends get right?

1. **They went to Job.** When they heard about Job's troubles, they went to him. Many people would not have. Many people don't. Pain is confusing, and most people don't want to touch it.
2. **They grieved with Job.** There was no debate that Job was suffering. It was evident to all of them. They wept and mourned with Job, actually tearing their robes and covering themselves in dust. In other words, they lowered themselves to be in a similar place of suffering to identify with their friend.
3. **They said nothing.** In the moment of pain, the person suffering just needs people to be there. Words are rarely needed. As was common practice in that day, they would not say anything until the person suffering spoke first. In this particular case, that would be seven days and seven nights.

Out the gate, Job's friends are getting it right! They're nailing it! They are doing what many others are unwilling to do. Not unlike Job's wife, these three friends had pure motives. Their hearts were broken for the pain that Job was suffering. Showing up, grieving, and listening are what friends should do for each other, especially in times of pain. This is a great example for all of us to follow!

But here's the problem. It would have been better for Job's friends to quit while they were ahead. When Job was ready to speak, they too were ready to speak! As Job begins to put words to his suffering, instead of just listening, his friends will now choose to join the conversation. And when they do, the words coming out of their mouths will only contribute to Job's pain. In Job chapter 3, we hear from Job about the inner pain he is going through. He talks about wishing that he had never been born (Job 3:3, 11). Job adds to that thoughts of seeing no light or hope in any of his suffering. The very things he had done to prevent suffering and pain—being faithful and offering sacrifices not only for himself but for his kids—was all for nothing. Job was now experiencing all the things he had feared could happen, and in the middle of them all he has no peace.

Three rounds of questions and conversations begin between Job and his three friends Eliphaz, Bildad, and Zophar. In fact, most of the book of Job is focused on these conversations. It's impossible to recap all of what is said between Job and his friends, so if you haven't already, I would recommend you read the book of Job yourself. But what you do need to know is how these conversations go. Essentially, Job's three friends make the argument that God is holy and just and orders the world according to right and wrong. God rewards those who are good and punishes those who are evil. The only conclusion that Job's friends can come to is that for Job to be experiencing all the pain that he's going through, he must be guilty of doing something wrong. That's the only conclusion that makes any sense to them!

The arguments of Job's three friends even build one upon the other. When one friend stops, the next starts, and it only goes from bad to worse.

The first friend, Eliphaz, argues that Job is suffering because he has sinned. What Job needs to do is go to God and plead his case: acknowledge that God is just and that he is in need of God's mercy and forgiveness for what he has done, whatever it might be. "But if I were you, I would appeal to God; I would lay my cause before him" (Job 5:8).

The second friend, Bildad, adds to that argument with the notion that Job is still sinning because He won't admit he sinned. He's basically asking Job how long he will go on like this—how long could he live in denial of what he'd done? "How long will you say such things? Your words are a blustering wind" (Job 8:2).

The third friend, Zophar, goes even farther by saying that Job's sin must deserve even more suffering than he's already experienced. He essentially tells Job that whatever he did or was doing, he deserved to be punished *more* than he already was; it was time to knock it off and ask forgiveness. "Yet if you devote your heart to him and stretch out your hands to him, if you put away the sin that is in your hand and allow no evil to dwell in your tent, then, free of fault, you will lift up your face; you will stand firm and without fear" (Job 11:13–15).

Well, thanks, guys, for showing up! With friends like that, I mean—really?

Life can seem so unfair and cruel at times, can't it? These three friends believe they're offering Job the help he needs by saying, "God is faithful and just. We don't know what you did wrong, but whatever it is, you're being punished! Repent so you can be healed." But that's not what God is doing at all! Job's three friends have drawn the wrong conclusion about why Job is suffering, and the advice they are offering him is completely wrong. Job's suffering was not punishment for anything he had done wrong. Job was suffering because of what he had done right.

Knowing he has done nothing wrong, Job argues back to his friends that he is innocent of all their accusations. "I say to God: Do not declare me guilty, but tell me what charges you have against me" (Job 10:2). As Job refuses to accept his friends' premise for why he is suffering, the temperature in their dialogue increases. The conversations get heated. At one moment, Job says to his friends, "You however, smear me with lies; you are worthless physicians, all of you!" (Job 13:4). Can you imagine being in the worst moment of suffering you have ever experienced, only to have your closest friends tell you that it's your fault that you're suffering? Or that you're not doing what you should be doing to help yourself? "If you would just repent of whatever you did wrong, then everything will be OK!" That's absurd! Is that how things actually go in life, especially in moments of pain?

WHEN FRIENDSHIPS GET PERSONAL

During many years of physical suffering, I have had many friends who knew what it meant to show up, grieve, and listen. My family and I would never have made it through all the difficulties without family and friends who understood what it means to be a friend to others who are hurting. My brother, who is a medical doctor, and my sister-in-law, a nurse, have spent many hours with me in several hospitals across the two states of Indiana and Ohio. Their medical background was of significant help as we navigated a whole new world to us. Have you ever tried to read doctor's notes or test results? Without their help, I'd have just handed over the information and gone with whatever I was told!

Others made meals, gave gifts, or knew what to say and do at the right time. When our kids were younger, we had many friends who took them in even at the last minute, with several unexpected trips to the hospital. We will always be grateful, and we recognize that we never would have made it through without their help and support.

But as was true for Job, on occasion we've experienced the well-meaning but ill-advised thoughts and opinions of others. When people can't make sense of what's going on, they start to make things up! And it seems that the closer the relationships, the truer this becomes. We live in the age of social media, asking for or receiving the opinions of others on almost anything going on in life. But does anyone really find this helpful? Often people mean well but have no idea what you're going through, let alone what you *should* do.

In my experience, I had very well-meaning people give me all kinds of terrible advice.

"I have a brother who has IBS and he drinks this concoction made of beets and roots. I know it can help you!"

"Have you ever had to have a colonoscopy? Those are the worst!"

"You know, they have an oil that I'm sure if you rub it on your stomach, it will completely take your issues away."

Contending with emotions similar, I'm sure, to what Job experienced, I wanted to answer:

"You don't know what you're talking about! IBS is bad, but this is much worse. Your miracle concoction will not solve my issues."

"I get colonoscopies routinely, and while they are bad, they are *not* the worst thing—trust me."

"You can take your oil and, well, you know …"

Now, I'm not questioning their motivation. They meant well. But their advice was not something I could follow or find helpful. In the same way, Job's friends meant well; they were just wrong. And Job, wisely, chose not to follow their advice. Good thing, too, because the ending of his story might have been quite different if he had. If Job had listened to the well-meaning advice of both his wife and his friends, he only would have compounded his suffering, concluding that he must have been the cause of his own pain.

When we get to the end of Job's story, which ultimately ends with Job's healing, the relationship Job has with his friends plays a crucial part. In Job 42:10, we're told that "after Job had prayed for his friends, the Lord restored his fortunes and gave him twice as much as he had before." Now, why do you think it was important that Job prayed for his friends? It's because Job understood the importance of what Jesus would later teach His disciples to pray: "Forgive us our debts, as we also have forgiven our debtors." If you want to forgive others their debts so you can be forgiven of yours, what do you have to do? You have to pray for them, just as Job did for his friends! It's not what you're going to want to do when you're in pain, especially when people—even friends—blame you for the suffering you're facing. You won't want to pray for them, and the only way to get through it is to remember all that you've been forgiven.

And in a twist of irony, we find out that God is exactly who Job's three friends thought He was! He is a God of justice. He does declare what is right and wrong. But while they thought Job was the one who was wrong, God tells them that they were the ones who were wrong.

> After the Lord had said these things to Job, he said to Eliphaz the Temanite, "I am angry with you and your two friends, because you have not spoken the truth about me, as my servant Job has." (Job 42:7)

I'm sure they didn't expect to hear that from God! And I'm quite certain what God says next caught them completely off guard.

> "My servant Job will pray for you, and I will accept his prayer and not deal with you according to your folly. You have not spoken the truth about me, as my servant Job has." (Job 42:8b)

In other words, "Job was right and you were wrong. I'm actually in conversation and relationship with Job and will listen to him, not you!"

Relational pain is extremely difficult, especially when compounded with any other pain you are experiencing. And while it won't seem fair, sometimes you will have to pray for others when they don't deserve it. When you do, just remember you are praying to your Father in heaven, who first forgave you.

Only in the closing verses of the book of Job will Job finally receive the comfort that he needs. And lo and behold, it comes in the context of relationships with others:

> All his brothers and sisters and everyone who had known him before came and ate with him in his house. They comforted and consoled him over all the trouble the Lord had brought upon him, and each one gave him a piece of silver and a gold ring. (Job 42:11)

Even when Job finally experienced physical healing, having his material wealth not only replaced but increased and his broken relationships restored, Job was still in need of comfort and support. He was still grieving and hurting from all he had gone through and in need of comfort. God designed us to need others, and in this moment of healing for Job, it was through relationships, even those that needed to be mended, that the comfort and support Job needed is finally provided.

Answering the question, "What's the plan?" must also include praying, "Forgive us our debts, as we also have forgiven our debtors."

CHAPTER 5

THE FINAL UNFAIR TEST

*And lead us not into temptation, but
deliver us from the evil one.*

MATTHEW 6:13 NIV

N ow, the only thing worse than having well-meaning friends offer bad advice or come to wrong conclusions in your season of pain is to have people you don't really know, people who have a lot less life experience—especially in the area of suffering you're dealing with—but who think they know it all, start speaking. As you read that, I'm guessing that somebody came to mind. Who was it? Maybe say a word of prayer for them before continuing to read.

As we get closer to the end of this book, I'm glad you didn't take my early warnings about the challenges of reading it, and I hope that by now you know my heart is one of concern, not condemnation. I want healing for whatever pain you're going through! Pain is never easy, and the solutions to it can be equally difficult. As the cliché goes, "Things often get worse before they get better."

Entering the story of Job at this point is an obscure character by the name of Elihu. While his appearance will be brief, it plays an important role in our discussion. The opening verses of Job chapter 32 pick up after the conversation among the three friends and Job that we discussed in the previous chapter and go on to shed some light on Elihu:

> So these three men stopped answering Job, because he was righteous in his own eyes. But Elihu son of Barakel the Buzite, of the family of Ram, became very angry with Job for justifying himself rather than God. He was also angry with the three friends, because they had found no way to refute Job, and yet had condemned him. (Job 32:1–3)

Elihu was a much younger bystander who had been listening in on the conversation between Job and his three friends (Job 32:6–7). And Elihu is angry with everybody! He's angry at Job. He's angry at Job's three friends for failing to convince Job of his sin, which, in all of their minds, is the cause of Job's suffering. Bottom line, Elihu is an angry young know-it-all! If you think I'm exaggerating, read Elihu's own words: "Be assured that my words are not false; one who has perfect knowledge is with you" (Job 36:4). What Elihu is saying is, "Have no fear, I am here! None of you seem to be grasping what God, the one who has perfect knowledge, has to say about all of this! So, I will be glad to explain it all to you!" It's one thing to think that, but how arrogant do you have to be to actually say it out loud?

Elihu's argument is very much like that of Job's three friends, but with one distinction. They all conclude that Job has sinned and is suffering because of it, and they believe all Job needs to do is repent, own what he has done, and seek forgiveness from God so that he might be healed. But here's the difference in Elihu's argument. Eliphaz, Bildad and Zophar argued that Job's sin is what caused his suffering in the first place; they're saying, "We don't know what it is you've done, but you did *something*, and you're getting what you deserve!" Elihu's argument is different; he's saying, "Job, you're actually sinning *because* of your suffering! Your pain, which we can all see you're going through, is what is causing you now to sin!"

Do you see the difference between the two arguments? Job's three friends have no proof or evidence that Job has done anything wrong, but they see his suffering as evidence that he has sinned. Elihu is saying, "We absolutely have proof and evidence of Job's sin! Just listen to how Job is speaking about his suffering. Job's suffering is causing him to sin! He takes no responsibility at all for what is happening!" At one point, Elihu says:

> "Job says, 'I am innocent, but God denies me justice. Although I am right, I am considered a liar; although I am guiltless, his arrow inflicts an incurable wound.'" (Job 34:5–6)

Another way to state Elihu's position would be that Job's not suffering because of his sin, he's sinning because of his suffering. In other words, Job's response to his suffering is what's causing him to sin!

Elihu will also make the argument that God uses suffering as a means of teaching and instruction, not just as punishment for sin (Job 36:10–11). If Job would just accept what is happening and trust in God, he might actually learn something! Elihu is suggesting that Job had become arrogant as he tried to defend his innocence. How ironic it is for Elihu to come to this conclusion? This advice from the guy who just told everyone, "Don't worry! I get what's really going on here. I will explain it all to you!" And Elihu simply can't take much more of Job's excuses and denials. How can Job respond to the Almighty God as he does? How can Job maintain his innocence in light of what seems so obvious to everyone else?

What is Job supposed to do with all of that? You might be thinking, "Job just can't catch a break," and you'd be right. Put yourself in Job's shoes for a minute. You've lost everything. You're as sick and near death as you've ever been. Three of your closest friends have arrived and drawn terrible conclusions about the suffering you're in, and now you have to listen to some young person who thinks he knows it all! How in the world did Job get through this moment?

I believe that Job understood what Jesus would later teach His disciples about praying: "And lead us not into temptation, but deliver us from the evil one" (Matthew 6:13). If Job ever needed to pray a prayer like this, it was at that moment. While not having sinned at all and in extreme pain and suffering, he's being told by others that everything he's experiencing is his fault! If he's not careful, Job will fall into sinning! It wouldn't be surprising if Job concluded, "Forget all of this! I have done nothing wrong! I don't care what everyone else is saying! I don't need this. I'm going to give up on everyone and everything, including God!" It doesn't take a lot of mental gymnastics to see how Job might land there. In fact, many believers throughout history, going through similar circumstances, have come to exactly that conclusion. The difference for Job is that he doesn't. After facing everything that he had and to now have to respond correctly to the accusations of Elihu, is truly the final unfair test for Job. He has endured enough. He deserves none of the suffering he's already experienced. So if the answer to suffering in this moment is more suffering, that truly seems unfair.

When Jesus tells his disciples to pray, "And lead us not into temptation," the word *temptation* actually means "test." As followers of Jesus, we will experience times of testing, and surprisingly enough God allows it! So you may be wondering, "Well, what's the difference, then, between temptation and testing? Why would Jesus ask His followers to pray 'Lead us not into temptation' if we're going to face times of testing anyway?" For now, let me say this: the pain you are suffering might be preparation for the plans God has for your life. There are things a follower of Jesus needs to understand that may not be possible without testing. We need to make an important distinction between "temptation" and "testing" as it relates to pain. Sometimes the pain we experience is giving into temptation that leads to sin so that we suffer the consequences of sin. Other times we experience pain because God is allowing us to be tested to make us into who He wants us to be.

I understand that this may be a painful reality to contemplate. But while painful, it is no less true. If Job didn't handle this moment carefully and correctly, if temptation had been allowed to grab hold and move him towards sin, the consequences would be enormous.

JESUS'S TIME OF TESTING

Two chapters before Jesus teaches the Lord's Prayer in Matthew 6, we find the story of how Jesus is tested in the wilderness. If you're in a season of testing, take some comfort that Jesus experienced this same kind of season Himself. The difference between Jesus and humankind is that Jesus was tested but never sinned. Everyone will be tested. No one is immune to it. Suffering periods of testing does not mean that you've done anything wrong! But unlike Jesus, we all have sinned. The challenge is to overcome the times of suffering with God's help, and avoid falling into sin. Sin is the moment we give into temptation and disobey God.

We also need to understand that Jesus was tested when He was most vulnerable. After fasting for forty days and nights, Jesus is in the desert and in a weakened state when Satan shows up to test him. He's tired, alone, and weak. I don't think it's too much of a stretch to compare the state he's in to that of Job when he faced his time of testing with Elihu. Matthew 4:1 tells us something else of great importance: "Then Jesus was led by the Spirit into the wilderness to be tempted by the devil." When people ask how God could allow Job to endure all the pain, suffering, and testing he went through, you only have to look at the life of Jesus for the answer. Does the Spirit leading Jesus into the wilderness mean that God was not caught off guard here? This time of testing for Jesus was all by design and purpose? The answer is yes! Just as with Job's time of testing, God was intimately involved and aware of everything going on. When you experience your own suffering and pain and wonder why, remember you are in good company. This may not be the one you would want, but it is one you can find comfort in: God allows testing for a reason. Jesus's testing in the desert ushers in His time of ministry here on earth. It wasn't an ordination service or a prayer of blessing. It was a time of testing.

So how does this time of testing go for Jesus? He will have to endure three different tests as part of His ordeal.

1. The test of daily bread. Matthew 4:3 says, "The tempter (Satan) came to him (Jesus) and said, 'If you are the Son of God, tell these stones to become bread.' " Remember back in chapter 3 when we talked about Jesus teaching us to pray "Give us today our daily bread"? It is no surprise that daily bread is one of the areas in which our enemy tests us and leads us into temptation. Jesus was famished, and He knew he could easily take care of that by snapping his fingers and turning stones into bread. But that's not what He does. Jesus's response is to quote God's Word from Deuteronomy 8:3. This passage of scripture is where God reminds the Israelites of how He had led them in the wilderness for forty years to humble and test them, causing them to hunger before providing manna for them.

> Jesus answered, "It is written: 'Man shall not live on bread alone, but on every word that comes from the mouth of God.' " (Matthew 4:4)

The answer to this test was for Jesus to hold true to the Word of God, not the lies of the enemy. The Word of God should always be more valuable to us than even food itself! If Jesus had done what Satan told Him to do, He would have been expressing doubt in His Heavenly Father's ability to meet His need.

God will always provide the daily bread you need. Jesus understood that and passed this first test with flying colors.

2. The test of His Heavenly Father. The second test Jesus has to face comes back to something else Jesus taught His disciples to pray, "Our Father in heaven, hallowed be your name" (Matthew 6:9).

> Then the devil took him [Jesus] to the holy city and had him stand on the highest point of the temple. "If you are the Son of God," he said, "throw yourself down. For it is written: 'He will command his angels concerning you, and they will lift you up in their hands, so that you will not strike your foot against a stone.'" (Matthew 4:5–6)

Here Satan quotes Psalm 91:11–12, suggesting that all Jesus need do is to claim the biblical promise that angels would keep God's Son from striking His foot against a stone. Surely a faithful Father would fulfill His promise? Satan actually tries to use God's Word against Jesus!

But what was Jesus's answer to the first test? Didn't Jesus just say, "Man does not live on bread alone, but on every word that comes from the mouth of God." How foolish does Satan think Jesus is in this moment? Seriously, trying to use God's Word against Jesus was the tactic he chose to go with? Now, if Satan tried this with Jesus, I'm quite confident he will think you and I are that foolish too. Your enemy will use God's Word *against you*. He's been doing that throughout history, he's doing this today in society at large, and he will do it in your life. Watch out!

What Satan is testing here is the genuine Father-Son relationship that Jesus has with God, His Heavenly Father. Satan would love nothing more than to undermine this relationship. He's tempting Jesus to put God in an unbelievable position to save His Son in this moment. If Jesus had thrown Himself off the top of the temple, and angels had come to attend on Him, that would have meant an end to His suffering. The angels certainly would have provided for His current physical needs. (Interesting to note, when all is said and done, angels do arrive to care for Jesus, in Matthew 4:11.) There's no doubt this was a tempting offer for Jesus. But if Jesus had done what Satan suggests, what would have happened when He goes to the Cross to die for our sins and God didn't intervene in that moment? Can't you imagine people saying, "Well, God saved His Son Jesus that time He threw Himself down from the temple, so why did He not save Him from crucifixion?" But if God saved Jesus from the Cross, it would be impossible for humankind to experience forgiveness; both cannot be possible. God saving His Son Jesus during His second test in the desert had the potential of creating confusion later when He doesn't rescue Him from crucifixion. If Jesus got this second test wrong, it would have undermined His relationship with His Heavenly Father by manufacturing a crisis at the direction of Satan and then expecting God, His Heavenly Father to do something about it. That is not how the relationship between God (Father) and Jesus (Son) was supposed to work.

So how did Jesus respond to this test? "Jesus answered him, 'It is also written: 'Do not put the Lord your God to the test' " (Matthew 4:7). Jesus again quotes God's Word, this time Deuteronomy 6:16, where God Himself told Israel they were not to put him to the test. We don't get to put God in an awkward place of testing, regardless of what pain we are experiencing. We don't get to reverse the test challenge back on God just because we don't like the time of testing we're facing! It doesn't work that way. This is how Satan has been trying to undermine the relationship between followers of God and their Heavenly Father throughout history.

Satan comes to us and says, "Ask God to take your pain away! He can heal you, so put Him on notice that that's exactly what you want Him to do. He can give you the job! He can make you rich! He can heal your relationships! He can cure your illness! Force God into position where He has to do something! In fact, tell others that that's exactly what He's going to do!"

But God is not a genie in the bottle to do what we want Him to do. The pain many people have experienced in life has come from

Satan's ability to win this battle in their life. It's why early on in the Lord's Prayer, we must pray, "Our Father in heaven, hallowed be your name" (Matthew 6:9). The testing you may be facing in your life just might be found in your personal relationship with your Heavenly Father. And before you pray, "Lead us not into temptation, but deliver us from the evil one," you better have prayed to your Holy Father in heaven. Do you see how this all must work together?

3. The test of taking shortcuts. After passing the first two tests, Jesus will face a final incredible test. Jesus has solidified that He trusts nothing and no one else for His daily provision. He has not allowed the enemy to undermine the relationship He has with His Heavenly Father. But now Jesus will face a test, not unlike the one that many followers of God have experienced. Will we accept not only God's plans and purposes but also the way in which God wants to work out those plans and purposes? This next test for Jesus has everything to do with learning to pray this part of the Lord's Prayer: "Your kingdom come, your will be done, on earth as it is in heaven" (Matthew 6:10). The final test that Jesus will have to endure goes like this:

> Again, the devil took him to a very high mountain and showed him all the kingdoms of the world and their splendor. "All this I will give you,' he said, 'if you will bow down and worship me." (Matthew 4:8–9)

All our enemy Satan wants is for us to acknowledge and worship him. All Jesus came to do was to rightly establish His kingdom here on earth. On the surface, this seems like a great business deal being hatched between Satan and Jesus. Both parties in the agreement will get what they want. Satan gets the recognition he so desperately desires, and Jesus can establish His kingdom without having to endure the pain of the cross. So what's the problem?

The problem has everything to do with shortcuts. God's kingdom being done on earth as it is in heaven must be accomplished in the way that God desires. End of negotiations. End of story. Jesus knew all of this. He knew exactly what Satan was up to. So how does Jesus answer this final test? By going back to God's Word and quoting Deuteronomy 6:13.

> Jesus said to him, "Away from me, Satan! For it is written: 'Worship the Lord your God, and serve him only.'" (Matthew 4:10)

Even when you've reconciled some large issues in your relationship with God, the temptation will always be to take shortcuts—to accomplish God's will but in a way that's easier, that makes more sense to us and comes with a lot less pain. We'll say things like, "God wants me to do something, but I'll just do it this way." Even when we set out to do something good, we can still give into temptation by choosing to do it the wrong way. Doing the right thing, the wrong way, is still wrong. If Jesus had taken Satan up on his offer, He might have established a political kingdom here on earth, but it would have stopped well short of the ultimate goal of establishing a way for people to be forgiven of their sins. There was no shortcut around the cross for Jesus in accomplishing this ultimate goal.

JOB'S NON-RESPONSE TO ELIHU

So what do you think happens next in the conversation between Job and Elihu? How does Job respond in this moment of temptation and testing? Does Job reply to Elihu in the same way he did to his three friends? Will Job continue to maintain his innocence in light of overwhelming evidence that would seem to suggest otherwise? Does anyone, including Job, actually respond to Elihu? The answer to this question might surprise you. The answer is no one. No one replies to Elihu. Not Job. Not Job's friends. Not even God Himself answered Elihu's accusations against Job. This must have come as quite a shock to someone who was so insistent on being right and heard as was Elihu! If Elihu was offended before, he must have been outraged now.

When you're in a time of testing and suffering, here's a piece of advice: some people in life are not worth listening to. The question always is whom to listen to about what? Don't fall prey to being an Elihu who thinks he knows it all, but don't listen to every Elihu who comes your way, either. Here's the other thing: don't listen to them, and don't respond to them. Some people are not worth responding to. Don't get into foolish arguments with people who don't understand what they're talking about or have any idea what you're going through. I know—this doesn't sound very Christian, right? Well, sometimes it's better to say nothing and walk away. If you engage, you may only increase your own pain and suffering.

TO OR NOT TO SPEAK

I've had a few Elihu moments along the way during my own journey. One Sunday over lunch, after preaching two services I was asked by someone who was new to the church, someone I barely knew, whether I was really sick or just a wuss. After many years of struggling physically, especially trying to get through Sundays, I found these moments difficult. Reacting inappropriately was not going to solve anything. I often had the thought, *Do I really have to deal with this?* Thankfully, with God's help, I was able to handle these situations and conversations, at least as best as I could.

Having said that, at least once I did not handle things well. One Wednesday night at a board meeting, I reacted all wrong. It would be fair to say that I wasn't hitting on all cylinders physically that night, but that was not a reason to react in the manner I did. I was angry and showed it. The details of the discussion are not important, but I had to go back to the board and apologize for how I responded.

Through the years, I have had to relearn how to interact with others when I chronically felt unwell. Sickness is no excuse to react poorly; however, it also does not come naturally to respond otherwise. I am sure many of us would admit to struggling with how to rise above comments, issues, or frustrations while not feeling well. In these moments, I have had to learn to pray immediately, "And lead us not into temptation, but deliver us from the evil one. If I have to face this testing on top of suffering, then please, Lord, lead me into responding correctly so I do not sin!"

The closer the relationships, the more this seems true. There have been several occasions when I've had to go back to either my wife or my kids and say, "I'm sorry. There is no excuse for how I reacted or what I said. Please forgive me." But it's also important not to keep responding that way and then asking for forgiveness. That's a dangerous cycle to fall into. How I was interacting with others had to change, despite the challenges of life. The constant asking for forgiveness, presuming on the good graces and understanding of others, could not become my default. "Oh, they'll understand because I don't feel well." I had to learn—and am still learning—to respond correctly so that temptation does not take hold, leading me to sin.

CONVERSATIONS TO HOLD ON TO

God has also been faithful to provide some helpful, practical, and important conversations along the way for me to hold on to. Many times you can begin to lose your mind or blame yourself for all the pain and suffering you're going through. It's easy to buy into the notion that somehow you contributed to your own suffering, especially if other well-meaning people are suggesting that possibility. I know that seems wild to suggest, but it does happen—just ask Job!

One such important conversation I had was with a gastroenterologist (GI) whom I saw at the Cleveland Clinic, the second-best hospital system in the US for GI issues. I have had three of my surgeries at the Cleveland Clinic. The medical advice and care I received has been from the top doctors in one of the nation's leading hospital systems. Early on in this process, meeting with this doctor at the Cleveland Clinic and being at a pretty low point, I asked him, "Was there anything I could have done to avoid all of this? Did I somehow contribute to the pain and suffering I've been experiencing?"

He was an incredibly friendly and kind doctor and simply said to me, "I've looked at your case, and what you're facing is always a problem. But you need to know that you did nothing wrong! There's nothing you could have done differently. Unfortunately, you've just had bad luck."

On the one hand, this was hard to hear, but on the other, it was rather comforting. At least I didn't somehow contribute to my own pain.

Temptation or Testing?

So what do we do when we're in the middle of pain and suffering and find ourselves dealing with temptation and testing? What happens when we pray, "And lead us not into temptation, but deliver us from the evil one," but still find ourselves facing temptation and testing? Is it right to pray this way if it's going to happen anyway?

Here's what I think you can conclude. If you pray this prayer and still experience trials and temptations, then you know that God is allowing this moment as a test to further train you up as a disciple of Jesus. You can take comfort and peace in the knowledge that just like Jesus and Job, you are experiencing a time of testing that God is allowing in your life. What you may never know are the other times of temptation you may have experienced if you had not prayed this prayer.

After you pray, "Lead us not into temptation, but deliver us from the evil one," there are two responses I would recommend when you still face a season of testing and have to interact with others, especially any Elihu who may come your way.

1. Just don't respond. This is the example of Job and Elihu. Pray, and walk away! Some of my best responses in interacting with others I didn't know very well were simply not to offer a response. Getting into it was not going to solve anything. This world is full of people who have no idea what they're talking about, especially as it relates to what you're going through. You don't need to engage them. Don't listen to them and don't respond to them. Pray for them.

2. Read God's Word. If you are going to respond, it should be at the leading of your Heavenly Father and based on His Word. I have had to learn that if I do respond, I'd better be on solid ground biblically, just like Jesus during His time of testing. Following are a few verses I have found helpful when I faced times of temptation and testing.

> Blessed is the one who perseveres under trial because, having stood the test, that person will receive the crown of life that the Lord has promised to those who love him. (James 1:12)

> When tempted, no one should say, "God is tempting me." For God cannot be tempted by evil, nor does he tempt anyone. (James 1:13)

> No temptation has overtaken you except what is common to mankind. And God is faithful; he will not let you be tempted beyond what you can bear. But when you are tempted, he will also provide a way out so that you can endure it. (1 Corinthians 10:13)

I also find great peace when I remember that Jesus endured the same types of testing we face and understands what we're going through. The writer of Hebrews reminds us:

> Because he [Jesus] himself suffered when he was tempted, he is able to help those who are being tempted. (Hebrews 2:18)

> For we do not have a high priest who is unable to empathize with our weaknesses, but we have one who has been tempted in every way, just as we are— yet he did not sin. (Hebrews 4:15)

Answering the question "What's the plan?" must also include praying, "And lead us not into temptation, but deliver us from the evil one."

CHAPTER 6

YOUR PAIN, GOD'S PURPOSE

*For thine is the Kingdom and the power,
and the glory, for ever and ever.*
MATTHEW 6:13B KJV

As we approach the final chapter of this book, an important person has yet to speak into the pain Job has been experiencing, raising an obvious question: where is God in all of this? What does He have to say about all that has happened? When we experience the pain of life, why is it that God's voice often seems to be the last one we consider? Why do we listen so much to the thoughts and opinions of others, especially during the most difficult moments of our lives? Could the argument be made that God actually decided to be silent during this time of suffering in Job's life? Whom was Job supposed to listen to? The only ones talking were these other people! Have you ever wondered why God has been so silent during your time of pain?

JOB'S CONVERSATIONS WITH GOD

When Job responded to his wife, his friends, and a complete stranger, what he may not have realized was that God was listening in. Job was not just talking to those standing in front of him; he was talking to God Himself. And what did God hear? God heard Job questioning God.

Here are some examples.

> After this, Job opened his mouth and cursed the day of his birth. He said: "May the day of my birth perish, and the night it was said, 'A boy is conceived!' That day—may it turn to darkness; may God above not care about it; may no light shine on it." (Job 3:1–4)

Suffering and pain will make you come to some pretty extreme conclusions! It's hard for Job to be too mad at his wife for expressing her feelings that he should "curse God and die" (Job 2:9) when he wishes he had never been born.

> "Oh, that I might have my request, that God would grant what I hope for, that God would be willing to crush me, to let loose his hand and cut me off! Then I would still have this consolation—my joy in unrelenting pain—that I had not denied the words of the Holy One." (Job 6:8–10)

If he had to have been born, then Job is now hoping that God will take him out, shorten his life, before he crosses the line of denying God. At least Job could still take pride in the reality that while God seems to have abandoned him, he has not abandoned God.

> "Although I am blameless, I have no concern for myself; I despise my own life." (Job 9:21)

We've all had moments when we've said things like, "I've done nothing wrong! Don't blame me! I hate my life!" When we say these things, we are questioning the God who gave us life in the first place—just as Job did.

But something interesting begins to happen in Job's life. As pain and suffering continue, Job's faith starts to regain some of its former strength. His tone begins to change:

> "Though he slay me, yet will I hope in him." (Job 13:15a)

> "I know that my redeemer lives, and that in the end he will stand on the earth." (Job 19:25)

Job's trust and faith in who God is begins to increase once again. In choosing the right response to God and his pain, Job will place himself on the road towards healing.

But let's not take for granted that Job responded the way he did. Job had a choice in all of this. He could either continue to trust God for what he can't figure out on his own, or go his own way. It's the same choice all those who suffer the pain of this life have to choose. But it doesn't mean that the questions Job has been asking about his suffering get answered. We might expect God now to answer Job's questions about why he has been suffering. If we were writing the story, that's probably how we would write it. Would you like to know how God finally answers Job? In a book that's forty-two chapters long, we don't hear from God until chapter 38.

> "Where were you when I laid the earth's foundation?" (Job 38:4)

> "Have you ever given orders to the morning, or shown the dawn its place?" (Job 38:12)

> "What is the way to the abode of light? And where does darkness reside?" (Job 38:19)

"Can you bring forth the constellations in their
seasons?" (Job 38:32)

"Will the one who contends with the Almighty
correct him?" (Job 40:2a)

God answers Job's questions, but with questions! The first
question God asks Job is, "Who is this that obscures my plans with
words without knowledge? Brace yourself like a man; I will question
you, and you shall answer me" (Job 38:1b–3). Another way God
might have asked this question is, "Who do you think you are?"
God is telling Job that he has no idea what he's talking about! His
words lack understanding of what is really going on.

Up to this point, God has been patient in listening to all Job's
questions, but now it's time for Job to be on the receiving end of
God's questions. It's OK to ask God questions. Just understand that
God may have some questions of His own. When God begins to ask
His questions, will you be able to answer them? And in all of this,
what God does not do is explain the reason for Job's pain. So guess
what? You may never know the reason for your pain, either!

I don't mean that you can't have confidence that your pain is
playing a part in God's greater plan and purpose. What I mean is
that you may not know all the specifics of why you are experiencing
the pain you are going through. In serving our Holy Heavenly
Father, at times we are on a "need-to-know" basis—and sometimes,
we don't need to know! It's above our pay grade.

I don't like that reality any more than you do. But reality is
reality. Truth is truth. What God is saying to Job is, "You didn't
create all of this! There's no way that you could possibly understand
all the things that are going on. Let me simplify things for you. You
don't need to know everything. You just need to trust everything to
me." And times of pain will clarify just how true that is.

So how does Job answer God? Here's what Job says: "Surely I
spoke of things I did not understand, things too wonderful for me

to know" (Job 42:3b). This is a huge moment in Job's relationship with God. Job has learned to trust God with what he does not understand, specifically the pain he has been suffering. That level of trust is only possible by going through the pain of life and knowing that God is still who He says He is and ultimately will do all that He said He would do. Pain does not mean that God has forgotten about you or is ignoring what you're going through. It might very well mean that God is working His plan and purpose out through your pain—your pain, God's purpose.

STORMS ARE NOT ALWAYS BAD

It's hard to talk about pain and not talk about storms. Storms play an important part in Job's story. Don't forget that a storm contributed to Job's suffering in the first place "when suddenly a mighty wind swept in from the desert and struck the four corners of the house" (Job 1:19) and caused the deaths of his sons and daughters. When Job was replying to his second friend, Bildad, and defending his innocence, he says that even if he called out to God and He actually responded, "He would crush me with a storm and multiply my wounds for no reason" (Job 9:17). There is no way Job would be a fan of storms! To Job, storms meant pain and suffering.

But when God finally speaks in all of this, we're told something amazing: "Then the Lord spoke to Job out of the storm" (Job 38:1a). Unless you already knew how the story of Job turns out, you were probably not expecting that. But the very thing—a storm—that contributed to Job's suffering is now the very thing that will lead to his healing. It is not out of character for God to be associated with storms. In scripture, God's presence is often associated with the whirlwind or storm. What better example of the power and might of God could there be than a storm? God took Elijah into heaven in a whirlwind (2 Kings 2:1–11), and Psalm 77:18 and Nahum 1:3 tell us that God's presence is in the whirlwind. God's coming is often referred to as a whirlwind (Isaiah 66:15; Jeremiah 4:13, 23:19). God appeared to Ezekiel in a whirlwind (Ezekiel 1:4).

In life, we are afraid of storms. We have sirens and other warnings to let us know that a storm is approaching. The news breaks into our favorite TV show or sporting event to bring us the latest on whatever storm is happening at that time. When I first moved to the Midwest from Canada, this was something I had to get used to. I was used to snow and shovels, but not tornado sirens and hunkering down in closets. Wrapping up his speech to Job, Elihu too notices that storm clouds are beginning to form, saying, "His thunder announces the coming storm" (Job 36:33a) and asking, "Do you know how God controls the clouds and makes his lightning flash?" (Job 37:15). It's almost as if Elihu is preparing the way for God to speak. And when God finally does speak, it is out of the storm.

I understand that when you see clouds starting to form, your first reaction might be to panic. Have you ever considered that maybe the exact opposite is about to happen? Maybe God is trying to get your attention because He now has something He wants to say! Once God has everyone's attention through a storm, He speaks.

THE FORGOTTEN LINE OF THE LORD'S PRAYER

The last line of the Lord's Prayer that many of us were taught to pray is, "For thine is the kingdom, and the power, and the glory, for ever. Amen" (Matthew 6:13b KJV). And just like God speaking out of a storm, this line of the Lord's Prayer is quite unexpected. It is not found in any of the modern translations we have for Matthew chapter 6, because when Jesus taught His disciples to pray the Lord's Prayer, He did not include this line in the prayer. It's just not there in the oldest manuscripts of the Bible for Matthew, chapter 6. This line does, however, appear in the King James Version (KJV). There are KJV purists who believe that there are no better translations, that the KJV is flawless and without any mistakes, so why the discrepancy?

If Jesus did not include this line when he taught the Lord's Prayer, should we include it today? Where did this line come from, and is it important?

There is a good explanation for why we should include this final verse of the Lord's Prayer when we pray. In fact, it's a rather powerful explanation. Let's do some further investigation into why.

First, all Jewish prayers concluded with a benediction or blessing, similar to the one in the KJV version of the Lord's Prayer. It wasn't necessary for Jesus to tell His disciples to use this phrase at the end of the Lord's Prayer because it was already a common practice for those who were Jews to do so. It was so prevalent that Matthew probably didn't feel it was even necessary to write it down. Matthew most likely concluded, "Of course the Lord's Prayer would end with these words! That's just how we already pray!" As time went on, the scribes who were charged with making copies of scripture naturally would have included this line as part of the prayer, even though Jesus, according to the oldest manuscripts, did not teach His disciples to say these words at the time.

To go a little deeper, this benediction or blessing may have originated from David's prayer in 1 Chronicles 29:11a. At the end of David's reign as king, as he is preparing for the building of the temple that his son Solomon would oversee, David prays this prayer:

> "Yours, Lord, is the greatness and the power and
> the glory and the majesty and the splendor, for
> everything in heaven and earth is yours."

You can hear the similarities to this Jewish benediction in "For thine is the kingdom and the power, and the glory, for ever and ever" (Matthew 6:13b KJV).

But long before King David's prayer in 1 Chronicles 29 or the Lord's Prayer in Matthew 6, Job understood the importance of God's kingdom being the first and foremost priority. When Job begins to answer God's questions, he replies

> "I know that you can do all things; no purpose of
> yours can be thwarted. You asked, 'Who is this
> that obscures my plans without knowledge?' Surely
> I spoke of things I did not understand, things too
> wonderful for me to know." (Job 42:1–3)

Beyond the pain and suffering of this life is God's kingdom, power and glory that is being established forever.

Your pain may actually be part of God's purpose. If you're going to have a proper answer to the question, "What's the plan?" you have to land this foundational truth. It's always about His kingdom, His power, and His glory. The problem with pain is that it causes us to become more consumed with our kingdom, our power, and our glory. But outside the purposes of God's kingdom, our pain simply does not make sense. If it's about our life, plans, and purposes, there simply is no room for pain. But once you've settled this issue related to God's kingdom and His will being done on earth as it is in heaven, then you also have to accept that God's will might include your pain. That may not be what you want to hear. It's beyond our human capacity to fully understand. But if God is working out the larger issues of life, than nothing is off the table, including our pain.

GOD'S PURPOSE IN MY PAIN

I always thought that the most powerful moments for me in ministry would come during times when God would work in positive ways. I imagined these times to include helping people one-on-one to understand who Jesus is and what He wants to do in their lives. I envisioned opportunities to speak, preach, and pastor, to do my part in kingdom work here on earth. It might even include influencing other leaders who could impact even more people. Isn't that what it means to be part of God's kingdom work here on earth? Wouldn't God's power and glory be best displayed that way?

But here's the truth. While I have enjoyed these kinds of seasons, there have been other, harder kinds of seasons that I never expected and that were much more difficult and painful—but seemed to have as much or more *kingdom* impact. I can't fully explain the reality that at times God works His purpose through our pain. Storms are not always a bad thing. Storms can bring pain, but they can also bring purpose. God's kingdom plans and purposes are larger than anything I can completely understand or possess the ability to wrap my mind around. The question is will I pray, "For thine is the kingdom and the power, and the glory, for ever and ever," only when things are going well? Or am I able to pray this final, forgotten line of the Lord's Prayer when all I can see are storms?

I began to understand this truth during one of my first (of many) stays in the hospital. If you're a patient who ends up having to be admitted for a prolonged period of time, who also has multiple issues involving more than one doctor, you will be assigned a case manager. Someone has to be able to coordinate the details among all the medical teams and groups involved in your care. Suffice to say, it can get complicated very quickly. One day my case manager came into my room to check on me. I had already been in the hospital for two weeks, so she was no longer a new face in the sea of new people I was meeting. She was very pleasant, good at her job, and I greatly appreciated the help and support she was providing.

On this particular day, as she came in the room, she dropped a pretty heavy binder into a chair, sat down in another chair, and said, "I know I'm supposed to check in on you, but you're a pastor, and I have some things going on in my life that I need help with. Would you mind if I talked to you for a minute?" I thought, *Well, I'm hooked up to all kinds of tubes and machines, so I'm not going anywhere! If she wants to talk, and if I can help, that is what I've been called to do.* I said a quick unspoken prayer that went something like, *God, I will trust that it's you that will speak through me and not all the drugs being pumped into me.* And for the next hour we talked. I listened to her story, shared what I felt led to share, and prayed that somehow God's kingdom plans and purposes would be done.

On another occasion, I was in Cleveland, having the most serious surgery I've had in this entire journey. It was a lengthy surgery that would remove my entire large intestine. All of it. During my time there, another nurse became an incredible help and support to both me and my wife Heidi. One day post-surgery, while recovering in the hospital, I was not doing well. I knew I was in rough shape, but apparently it was worse than I realized. Blood transfusions were involved. As she was leaving the hospital, a code came over the speaker for her floor indicating that an emergency response was needed. Someone was in a life critical condition, and she was convinced it was me because of how I had been doing that day. She quickly came back in tears but was relieved to learn that it wasn't me or one of her patients, though of course she was concerned that another patient on the floor was not doing well.

As I got closer to recovery, this same nurse asked if there was anything she could bring me. Was there anything I enjoyed eating that might help as we returned home to Indiana? At that time, I was kind of into Bob Evans' mashed potatoes (for whatever reason—don't you judge me!). Right before I was discharged, she brought me a gift to take home. Know what it was? A box of Bob Evans' mashed potatoes. Now, she didn't have to do that, and it wasn't about the potatoes. (It's never about the potatoes.) She had connected with not only me but my wife Heidi and some of our other family and friends who were with us during that time. In her own words, she expressed how our ability to handle a significant and serious life event had been an encouragement to her. In some mysterious way that truthfully only God can really make sense of, I believe God was using my pain for His kingdom's purposes.

I don't know how all these stories end, but I do believe that for whatever brief period of time God allows our pain to intersect the lives of others, His will is being done. Since that time, and after many more medical appointments, surgeries, and hospitalizations,

God seems to continue using the pain I've experienced in the lives of others.

Several years ago, I was in downtown Indianapolis at University Hospital, at yet another doctor's appointment, when I got a call from someone in our church. She wondered if I could go downtown to Riley Children's Hospital to talk and pray with a relative of hers whose child was having a GI surgery similar to one I had. The surgery was going to be done that day. I told her I was already downtown at the hospital right next door to Riley Hospital, and as soon as my appointment was over, I would head over to be with them. God's plan? God's timing? Circumstances being orchestrated at His control? How do you make sense of things like this?

As a pastor, I have found myself in the hospital rooms of many other people throughout the years. Nothing prepared me for these moments as much as being a patient myself. Not Bible college. Not seminary. Not even being a pastor before being a patient. Before I was a patient, I hated hospital visits. What do you say to people in difficult moments, facing unexplainable sickness? How do you navigate this world? Today, in a weird way, being in a hospital feels like familiar territory. I know how to navigate that world.

Once my brother had to take me back to the hospital. As I was being taken up to a room in a wheelchair, many nurses, techs, and other hospital employees were greeting me with, "Hey, Brad! What are you doing back? Are you OK?" My brother, who is a doctor in the same group as this hospital, was like, "Do you know everybody here?" Not everybody, but a lot! This was my Norm at Cheers moment (for you children of the eighties comedy), where everybody knew my name.

I could offer other examples of people God has brought to my path who have experienced or are experiencing physical issues similar to those I have had to face. I've been able to offer help and recommendations on what is a confusing journey for those who have never been on it. More important, it has given me an inroad into conversations at the spiritual level and the opportunity to pray for those who are suffering their own pain.

There have been many times when I've said to God, "I see what you're trying to do, but is there not a better way to do all of this?" And it's in that moment that I have to pray this final line of the Lord's Prayer: "For thine is the kingdom and the power, and the glory, for ever and ever." My pain, Your purpose. Your kingdom, Your power, Your glory. Forever.

Answering the question "What's the plan?" ends by praying, "For thine is the kingdom, and the power, and the glory, for ever. Amen" (Matthew 6:13b KJV).

CONCLUSION

So let me leave you with a question. I'm not asking whether you can steward the blessings of God in your life. I'm asking, can you steward the pain God allows in your life? The whole story of Christianity and of faith in Jesus is rooted in pain finding its purpose in God. The Old Testament prophets had to discover this. Jesus Himself is the ultimate example. Jesus's disciples' earthly lives did not improve when they came to faith in Jesus. So where did we get the idea that following Jesus will not involve pain? It's the one thing Jesus promised we *would* experience!

Here's what Jesus said in John 16:33b: "In this world you will have trouble. But take heart! I have overcome the world." We read that and think, "That's great for the characters in the Bible. That's great for Jesus. But I have bigger and better plans! I have a better way of getting the message out!" And you don't. You just don't.

But I want you to catch something incredibly important. Jesus promised that we would have not only pain in this life but something greater. Right before Jesus says that "in this world, you will have trouble," He promises the very thing we all need when the pain of life catches up with us. It's not only something everyone wants; it's something everyone can have.

Listen to these words of Jesus: "I have told you these things, so that in me you may have peace" (John 16:33a). While it may seem cruel that trouble and pain are a part of this life, only a loving God would promise that we could have His peace through it all. Jesus doesn't leave us hanging in relation to pain. He shows us how to have His peace while experiencing our pain. And there is no better example of someone who understood both the pain of life and God's peace than the one Job provides.

Read these words of James about Job:

> As you know, we count as blessed those who have persevered. You have heard of Job's perseverance and have seen what the Lord finally brought about. The Lord is full of compassion and mercy. (James 5:11)

I love how the New Living Translation puts it: "We give great honor to those who endure under suffering." (James 5:11a NLT).

I'm still learning every day what stewarding the pain of life really means. As I write this, I have no employment or ministry. I still have constant doctor's appointments and daily medical things that have to happen. But here's what I do know: I pray the Lord's Prayer first thing in the morning and the last thing at night. Depending on the day, I'll camp out in one part of the prayer over another. But as I do, I am reminded why Jesus gave us this prayer in the first place. It answers the question "What's the plan?" when I can't make sense of things.

I don't know what you're going through or what pain you're experiencing, but there is a plan. Job lived it. Jesus prayed it. And if you're willing, you can experience life and His peace in the middle of your pain.

WHEN THE LORD'S PRAYER BECOMES PERSONAL

Just like life, the prayer that Jesus' taught His disciples to pray is alive, moving, and breathing through all the ups and downs, challenges and celebrations, pain and peace that we face in this life. At some point, praying this prayer must move past reciting the words to embracing how personal they can be as you walk through life. For whatever season you may be in, the more personal the Lord's Prayer becomes to you, the more powerful its impact will be.

I would like to close by praying the Lord's Prayer in a way that I have prayed it many times. My intention is not to add to the words that Jesus taught His disciples to pray, but to show how personal they can become.

Our Father in heaven, hallowed be your name ...
Heavenly Father, you are Holy. There is none like you. You understand what I will never know. I'm so grateful that you are my Father, who loves me and knows exactly all that I'm facing and who is willing to walk beside me through everything I'm experiencing right now.

Your kingdom come, your will be done, on earth as it is in heaven ...
I am fully committed to your kingdom's will being done here on earth as it is in heaven. Whether that means good times or difficult times, blessing or suffering, wellness or pain, I fully trust that you are working out your kingdom plans through my life here on earth.

Give us today our daily bread ...
You know my needs for this day. Thank you for providing each day for all that I need. Show me what you would like me to do to participate with you in this provision. May you receive all the honor and glory.

Forgive us our debts, as we also have forgiven our debtors ...
Thank you for paying a debt I could never pay. I'm so grateful that my sins have been forgiven. Help me offer the same grace and mercy you have shown me to others.

And lead us not into temptation, but deliver us from the evil one ...
When life is more than I can handle and beyond what I can bear, help me remember that you are with me. You will not let me face

anything that I cannot handle with your help. Teach me what you want me to learn. Protect me from straying into areas you do not want me to go. Provide your strength where I am weak.

For thine is the kingdom, and the power, and the glory, for ever. Amen. No matter what I face today, whether it's pain or blessing, let me never forget that it is all about you. Your kingdom, through your power and for your glory, forever.

Printed in the United States
by Baker & Taylor Publisher Services